CLOTH
100 Artists

CLOTH
100 Artists

Contemporary & Heritage Techniques

LENA CORWIN

ABRAMS, NEW YORK

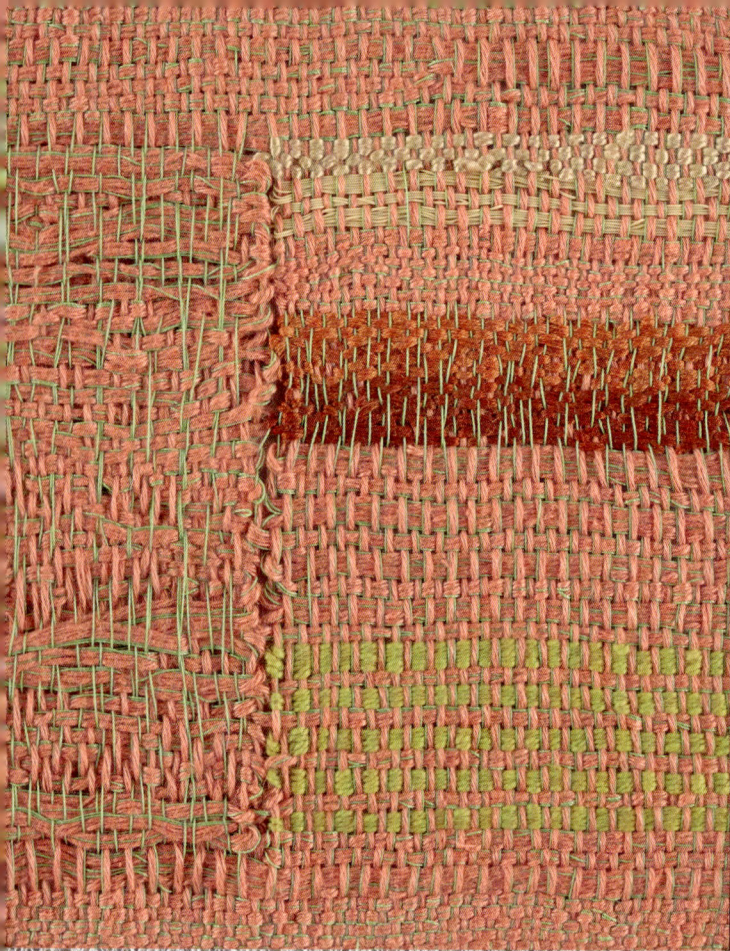

Contents

Introduction

I have been fortunate to follow my varied interests under the large canopy of art and design, and in the variety, a clear and constant through line has been working with cloth. As I began this book, I questioned why. Exploring my own dedication to cloth by connecting with kindred individuals has been deeply fulfilling. I've shared conversations with one hundred artists, often hearing their experiences reflected in my own.

Everywhere humans live, incredible historic cloth traditions exist and are continuing today. From swaddling blankets to burial shrouds, people live with cloth daily and for the entirety of their lives. I've framed the book within the parameters of living North American artists: one continent. With that framework, it became hard to narrow down the group to just one hundred. A core value in my research process has been curiosity and respect for handwork. I'm interested in the full range and want to hear the stories of makers, craftspeople, fine artists, and outsider artists. I look at their output with matching fervor, and I want to hear their stories.

My favorite realm has always been the place where craft and art start to merge. I love to see a framed quilt on a wall—a practical bedcover now viewed differently. Lenore Tawney is considered a groundbreaking artist in the elevation of fiber and craft to "fine art" status (she died at age one hundred in 2007). But in some art spaces, a hierarchy of perceived value remains.

In making this book and using "artist" with conviction for other people, I've warmed to using it myself with my own identity. Zak Foster (page 123) identifies as a "custodian of traditions," and I feel that too. I asked each artist in the book for words that describe their identity, and they responded—female, male, cisgender, nonbinary, queer, Black, Korean, Native, Mexican, Asian Pacific Islander, Nigerian, Japanese, Hawaiian, Buddhist, mother, educator, creative director, and many more.

In talking about her Mexican identity, Tanya Aguiñiga (page 179) says, "Learning about fiber, fabric, and textiles helps me take ownership of how I present myself to the world. It can offer different possibilities: generative space and power over my own identity. For a lot of us that are marginalized or seen as others, we can explore different ways of telling our stories."

Early on, I had a conversation with Kenya Miles (page 225). She expressed her desire to see a diverse representation of folks working with cloth, which, she felt, had yet to be present on bookshelves today. I agreed and, in my notes, I wrote, "I want to highlight work from deeply passionate people who offer different perspectives."

After decades of admiration and respect for the quilters of Gee's Bend, talking with Doris Pettway Mosely (page 85) was a special conversation for me. She called from her kitchen, and the conversation flowed from favorite recipes to the weather in Alabama. When I asked who in her life (living or past) encouraged her work with cloth, she swiftly responded, "My mother. She made quilts out of old clothes to keep us warm."

Another meaningful conversation I had was with Debra Sparrow (page 31). Sparrow works in traditional Salish weaving. She explained to me that "Salish weaving was essentially gone for eighty-five years." There were no living weavers to teach a new generation; the last known weaver before the revival was Sparrow's great-grandmother. Sparrow and a small group of women have brought it back. She feels a deep connection to her ancestry, pre-contact from Europeans. She says, "When I stand in front of my loom, I'm with them. I'm not here anymore. I'm back in time and they're whispering to me and guiding me."

Cloth plays a prominent role in my own family heritage, and, in my own way, I went into the family business. My maternal great-great-grandparents Lena and Wolf Seitchik moved from Kiev, Ukraine, to Philadelphia in 1907. Like many Jewish immigrants, my family members arrived in the United States to work in the schmata business—the Yiddish word for rag or cloth. Previously a tailor, Wolf opened a garment company manufacturing men's suits. My grandfather, uncle, and father continued in the field. Later, my father and uncle helped me land my first non-retail job, as an assistant for a French denim brand, where I really began learning about cloth production.

Working for big fashion brands in my twenties felt like an immersive and intensive textile course. I learned about every type of knit and woven fabric in their libraries of swatches. I worked with dozens of methods of fabric adornment, including embroidery, flocking, beading, transfers, studs, buttons, sequins, water-based ink, plastisol ink, discharge print, dip dye, and overdye.

After years working for large companies, I left to find more balance. I wanted to use my hands more, off the computer. I started personal and client projects, and teaching classes in my studio. Through the classes and freelance work, I connected with others who were passionate about cloth, by way of printing, sewing, quilting, dyeing, knitting, crocheting, felting, weaving, embroidery, or a combination of the above. I had the opportunity to write two instructional craft books during those years; Printing by Hand and Made by Hand.

Ten years later, with this book, I knew I wanted to go broader, zooming out to see a context for and deeper meaning in my passion. A list of artists grew, and chapters took shape naturally: Sew & Quilt, Weave & Braid, Print & Dye, and Loop & Felt. Most of the featured artists work with multiple techniques, but primarily one. Some, like Debra Weiss (page 149), were hard to place into one section because their work is so varied. Others, like Christy Matson (page 25), work almost exclusively with one technique they have extensively honed.

In conversing with each artist, I asked them about their family connection to cloth and who has supported their work. Most talked about their parents, grandparents, and greater family, but some have no family history of which they're aware, and instead found influence and support through teachers and chosen family. All contemporary cloth work builds on ancestral skills and methods developed around the world. It's so important to acknowledge influence from prior artists and cultures—whether our own culture or not—as we create new work.

As I researched the book and filled the gaps in my own knowledge, I discovered so many details and pieces of information I wanted to share: Each chapter begins with these notes, which are not aimed at being entirely comprehensive but are the definitions, traditions, and details I found most compelling and contextual. Chapters end with two instructional projects, each one an exercise in playing and experimenting with cloth by reusing items on hand or easily available (like old T-shirts, discolored cloth napkins, scrap fabric, and collected plant material). For these projects the goal is not a finished product but instead the process: taking time to play with ways to manipulate cloth and observe the results without a lot of judgment as to whether it was "successful." To everyone reading, I hope you are inspired to make room in your life to engage in work with cloth and with your hands.

Thank you to the one hundred artists for sharing your incredible work with me!

With gratitude,

Lena

Weave and Braid

Over, Under

WEAVING is a process of overlapping materials to make a new intertwined material. Woven cloth is made by interlacing two sets of yarns so they cross each other, usually at a ninety-degree angle. Very basic weaving can be done with materials alone; however, most often a weaver uses a loom—an apparatus that holds the threads in place. There are many types of looms, ranging from handheld to enormous industrial looms. The most common loom types are: backstrap loom, tapestry loom, inkle loom, rigid heddle loom, table loom, floor loom, and industrial loom. Looms are set up with lengthwise yarns called "warp" and crosswise yarns called "weft." Most woven cloth is made with the outer edges finished, and these ends are called "selvages" (running lengthwise, parallel to the warp yarns). The pattern in which the yarn interlaces determines the type of weave. The three basic weaves are plain, twill, and satin. More complex weaves, like pile, Jacquard, dobby, and leno, require more complicated looms or special loom attachments. Looms have been, and continue to be, tools with endless possibilities for the weavers who use them.

Weaving Traditions

Weaving in North America began, as it did in other parts of the world, with the prehistoric ancestors of native tribes. Early humans developed the first thread, made with handfuls of plant fiber that were stretched, pulled, and twisted together. The ability to produce thread was the starting point for the development of spinning, weaving, and sewing cloth. These same methods are used today, and the fundamental aspects of handweaving have remained unchanged.

Hopi and Navajo cultures are known for their masterful weaving. The Navajo tribe settled in what is now the Southwest United States in 900 CE. (They were previously nomadic.) A sedentary life brought agriculture and deeper development of craft skills. Woven cloth is, and was, an integral part of Hopi religious observances, rites of passage, and gift exchanges. The Zapotec people, native to the state of Oaxaca, Mexico, are well known for their graphic rug weaving and have a history of weaving dating back to 1500 BCE (possibly as early as 7000 BCE). The Huichol tribe in the Sierra Madre mountains of western Mexico create distinct, delicately patterned weavings, and much of their culture and way of life has been preserved because of their isolated location and resistance to assimilation. Up north in what is now the Vancouver, Canada, area, the Coast Salish people, ancestors of the Musqueam nation, had a rich weaving culture for thousands of years prior to European contact. During the 1700s, European inventors steadily mechanized spinning and weaving, ushering in the industrial revolution. During the Revolutionary War, Americans could not buy English goods, so domestic weaving became a necessity and dozens of weaving factories opened, using new mechanized looms. Frenchman Joseph Marie Jacquard patented the Jacquard loom (a loom controlled by a punch card machine) in 1801 and further contributed to the transformation of textile weaving, which shifted from the hands of skilled family weavers to mass production on an industrial scale. Christy Matson (page 25) talks about using a Jacquard loom: "I work back and forth between very analog materials, whether that is physical yarn itself that I paint on or marks that I make on paper. I then use a lengthy digital process to make a physical object with a tangible presence that functions both like a painting and like a textile, with all the history of both mediums, and an awareness of modern tools and computer processes."

BRAIDING. Similar in essence to weaving, braiding is a process of joining linear material by moving strands over and under each other in a pattern. Braiding differs from weaving in that the threads are not interwoven at right angles to each other but are instead crossed over. Braiding techniques include fingerloop, kumihimo, and lucet braiding. Fingerloop braiding (also called plaiting) can be done with three or more strands, ranging from simple to more complex. The art of macramé is similar to braiding but involves knotting the strands. Kumihimo braiding (a Japanese art of braiding) translates to "gathered threads" and requires a takadai loom. For lucet braiding, a wooden lucet tool is used to create a figure eight motion with the thread. Lucet braiding dates back to the Vikings and medieval period.

Braiding Traditions

Early humans developed ways to bind and bundle plant fibers and vines, creating braiding techniques that advanced over time across cultures. Palm leaves were braided into flat textiles in ancient Egypt. Andean braids were established circa 800 BCE. The Navajo braided horsehair rope, and the Hopi made cotton braided sashes with long fringes, called "wedding" or "rain" sashes. The Japanese art of kumihimo braiding, mentioned above, has been practiced for more than 1,300 years. In the 1800s, rug braiding became popular in the eastern United States. Braids were made out of scraps from the new machine looms, making round and oval rugs from braided strips sewn together in a spiral. Braided rugs were first mentioned in the *New England Farmer* newspaper in 1822. Braiding has been, and still is typically, a child's first learned method of interlocking fibers.

Alice Adams

Bronx, New York, and Linlithgo, New York
b. 1930

"The different places I've lived (or visited) have inspired me the most. I'm inspired by memories of where I grew up in Jamaica Estates in Queens, which was not like it is today. My father built our house in 1928, and there may have been another house down the road, but it was mostly woods at that time, and we were able to wander around and find wildflowers in the woods or play on a big fallen tree. After I graduated from Columbia, I had a grant to go to Aubusson, France, for a year to study tapestry-making, and that was a life-changing experience. I'd never been away from home; that whole year was different and had an enormous effect on me. I visited many Romanesque churches and their frescoes and a Corbusier building, Notre Dame du Haut at Ronchamp."

Interview by Jonathan D. Lippincott
for the American Abstract Artists organization, May 1, 2022

Born in New York City, Alice Adams is known for her weavings, sculptures, and public art projects. She studied painting at Columbia University and tapestry weaving at L'Ecole Nationale d'Art Decoratif. After completing her studies in France, Adams returned to New York with a tapestry loom to weave her own designs. Her practice departed from traditional tapestry technique, and she began creating woven patterns on a larger scale. Working on what conventionally had been the back of the tapestry, she developed surface articulation and added materials like rope, sisal twine, and found objects to the traditional wool and cotton surface. She moved weaving off the loom and into the realm of three-dimensional form. Her early work in tapestry, and in woven forms especially, was important in the American fiber art movement.

Brent Wadden

Vancouver, Canada, and Berlin, Germany
b. 1979

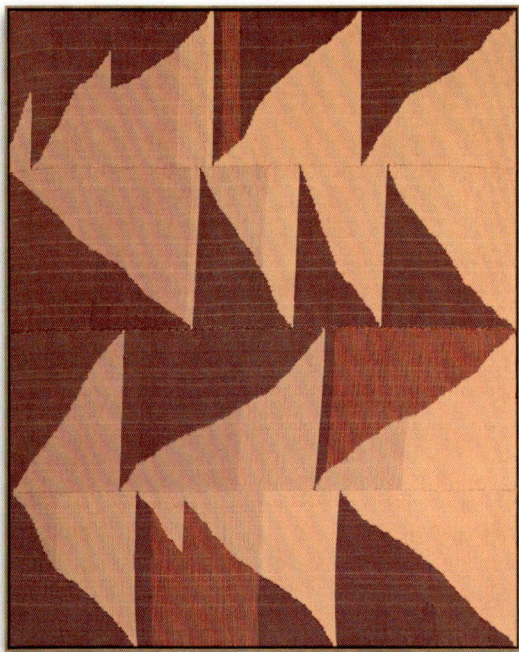

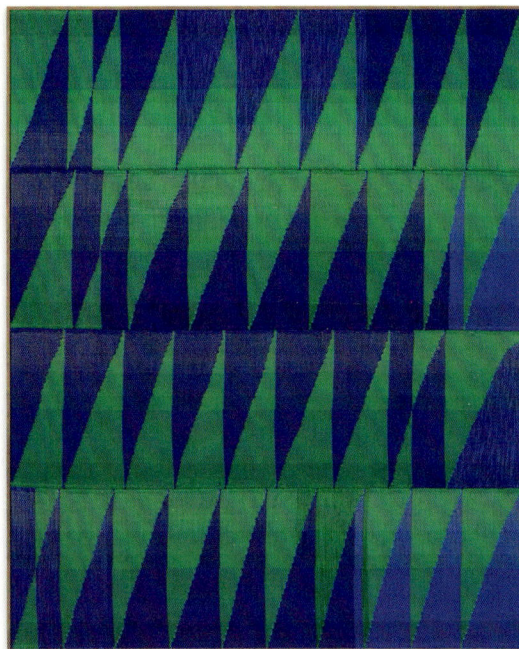

OPPOSITE
Avocado Salmon,
2015
Handwoven fibers:
wool, cotton,
and acrylic;
107 × 82 × 2 inches
(272 × 208 × 5 cm)

ABOVE LEFT
Alignment #33, 2013
Handwoven fibers:
wool, cotton,
and acrylic;
88 × 72 × 2 inches
(224 × 183 × 5 cm)

ABOVE RIGHT
Untitled, 2020
Handwoven fibers:
wool, cotton, acrylic;
67 × 56 × 2 inches
(163 × 142 × 5 cm)

"I grew up in a small working-class town during a time of economic decline. My family was thrifty by necessity, and that has stuck with me—sourcing most of my material secondhand. I work best when I have random materials on hand and let them guide what I make; the materials dictate what is possible. My work is about patterning, and rhythm, and embracing mistakes when they inevitably happen.

"Travis Meinolf (who lived around the corner from me in Berlin) gave me some intro [weaving] lessons. I took things slowly and approached the process as naively as possible; I thought doing things properly would take away from the final results. I worked for many years on the backstrap loom before buying my first floor loom."

Brent Wadden was born in Glace Bay, Nova Scotia. He earned his BFA from Nova Scotia College of Art and Design, where he studied under the late conceptualist painter Gerald Ferguson. Wadden originally focused his art practice on colorful, tessellated paintings and drawings. In 2010, he began working on a weaving loom. He often sources his materials pre-used and secondhand. Imperfect, intentionally mismatched panels, varying fibers, and pilled fabric all point to the hand rather than machine labor. Through warp and weft, Wadden's practice embraces the variations and glitches that emerge through a process of repetition, revealing subtle disruptions in the accumulation of line, color, and form. His abstract woven works bring together traditions of painting, design, craft, and folk art.

Carolina Jiménez

Brooklyn, New York
b. 1991

OPPOSITE
Winter's Sunset by the Cliffs, 2021
Silk dyed with avocado and black tea, linen, and indigo-dyed cotton; 35 × 47 inches (89 × 199 cm)

ABOVE
From Our Window on Chauncey, 2023
Silk dyed with avocado and black tea, and linen; 35 × 59 inches (89 × 150 cm)

"Weaving feels rooted in a particular craft tradition. And even though I'm using a different loom than what is used in Chiapas (a backstrap loom tied around the waist or two-pedal rug looms), it still feels like I'm tapping into it. I'm trying to learn what I can from that tradition, even though I'm separated from it, which is a larger part of the story of how I am connected to this thing that is not really mine. It's finding this strange in-between space."

Carolina Jiménez calls her woven works "monuments" to memory, bodies, and daily life. Many of her pieces incorporate Oaxacan cotton dyed with pigments from tea, cochineal, avocados, and other natural materials. Growing up in San Diego, Jiménez and her parents visited family in Mexico every other year (Chiapas and Mexico City). Her work develops through a process of both free experimentation and careful planning. From afar, the shimmering materiality and bold geometry are reminiscent of color-field abstraction. Influenced by her background in architecture, her woven paintings reflect a careful calibration of size and scale. She weaves on a Macomber loom in her home studio.

Cassandra Mayela Allen

Brooklyn, New York
b. 1989

"I love the malleability of fabric and the possibilities it brings as a material. I'm also fascinated by its relationship to our bodies, as 'second skins' or outlets of expression via the clothes we wear and as nurturing artifacts. I'm a very tactile person; I think touch is my most precious sense, so I think this is why I have chosen to work with fabrics. They invite you to touch."

Cassandra Mayela Allen was born and raised in Venezuela. Her parents owned a clothing brand when she was very young, and she has memories of the fabric, machines, threads, and colors. Since her forced migration from Venezuela in 2014, Mayela has lived in New York City. Her personal experiences have shaped her curiosity about the storytelling capacity of clothing and how migration affects feelings of identity and belonging.

Her work is largely community-oriented, exploring ways cloth and clothing are in relationship with one's perception of self. Her project *Maps of Desplazamiento* studies Venezuelan migration and how identity is shaped by the things we carry and the places we occupy. Using items of clothing as thread to reflect migratory history, she is building "maps" that unite Venezuelans in the current reality of their exile.

Christy Matson

Los Angeles, California
b. 1979

"The paternal side of my family lineage traces back to Sweden and Norway; my grandfather was born in British Columbia, and my father was born in southern Oregon. Meanwhile, my mother's family arrived on the West Coast two generations earlier, migrating from Oregon up to Anchorage, Alaska. Within the context of these long journeys, handmade functional textiles are one of the few items that have endured. From meticulously crafted quilts to tablecloths that bore witness to countless meals, and even delicate lace handkerchiefs, [each] feels replete with stories I'll never know. I only own a small number of these items, but they remain one of the only tangible connections I have to my ancestry, and they are the lens through which I understand that history."

Among Christy Matson's earliest memories involving art is sewing fabric collages using snippets from her childhood basement in Seattle. Her first sewing machine belonged to her grandmother, who graduated from the University of Washington in 1936 with a degree in textiles. The discovery of that machine (at age seven or eight) sparked Matson's love of both cloth and mechanical machines. Today, Matson's woven, wall-mounted works combine the skill, sensitivity, and craft of painting and handweaving with the artist-directed process of an industrial Jacquard loom. Matson begins her process with watercolors, ink drawings, collages, and other works on paper. She then uses a digital process to translate these compositions into instructions her loom can understand, and, as she works the machine, she improvises on the weft (horizontal rows) with creativity and nuance.

Clare Hu

Brooklyn, New York
b. 1996

OPPOSITE
9500 Medlock, 2023
(detail)
Overshot weave
(Lee's Surrender)
Digital images
printed on cotton,
and chiffon,
duck cotton, and
hardware;
89 × 57 inches
(226 × 145 cm)

ABOVE LEFT
Prospective Patch 11,
2023
Triple weave, painted
warp, digital image
on fabric, thread,
duck cotton;
55 × 38 inches
(140 × 97 cm)

ABOVE RIGHT
Prospective Patch 11a,
2023
Triple weave, painted
warp, digital image
on fabric, thread, and
duck cotton;
60½ × 48 inches
(154 × 122 cm)

"For me the practice of weaving is always evolving, and I learn so much with every project I do. There's a lot of frustration and boredom that can happen, but I think working through the process and spending the time doing it gives me an appreciation and a connection to a larger lineage of weavers and to my own family history."

"I never had a strong connection to making textiles or creating cloth growing up, but I did have an attachment to old clothing from family, or blankets and quilts gifted from family members. That feeling of connectedness through the tactility of textile objects is something I try to re-create in my own work."

A sense of the South runs through Clare Hu's work, informed by her birthplace, Atlanta, Georgia. She focused on fiber and material studies at SAIC (School of the Art Institute of Chicago). Hu explores how Southern myths are acted and reenacted in the stories and objects surrounding them. She describes her work as a three-sided negotiation of nostalgia: the myths of Southern nostalgia, her own nostalgia for the Atlanta community of her childhood, and a "ghost nostalgia" for the tight-knit Chinese community her parents experienced in the 1970s. Digital photography integrated into her weavings consists of landscapes around Atlanta: suburban strip malls, fragments of businesses in traditionally Chinese communities, and symbols of the South's Confederate past. Sometimes she cuts up older work and reweaves it into new work. The fabric warps, stretches, and pulls, creating a tension between what is revealed and what is guarded.

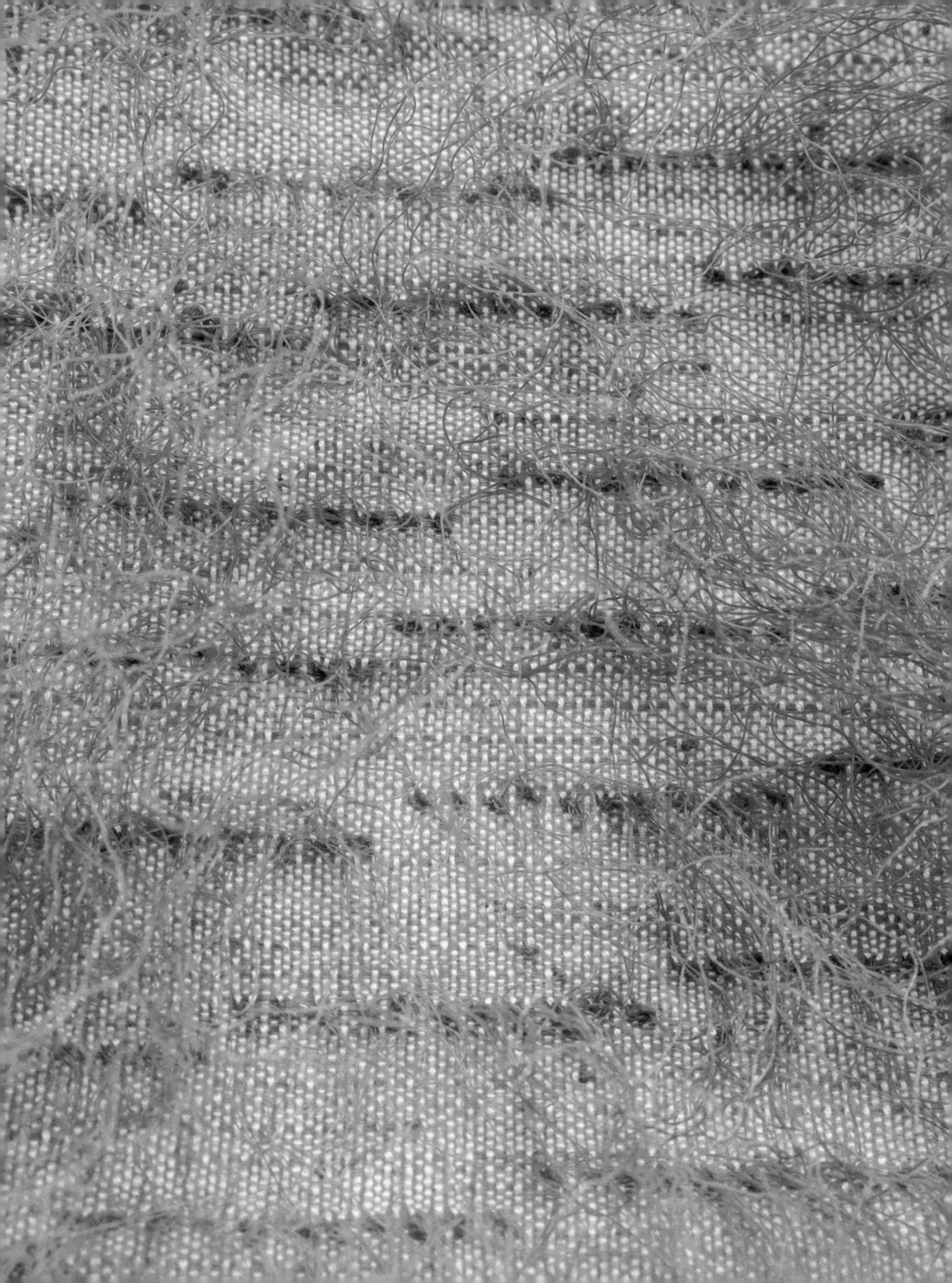

Dana Haim

Miami, Florida
b. 1983

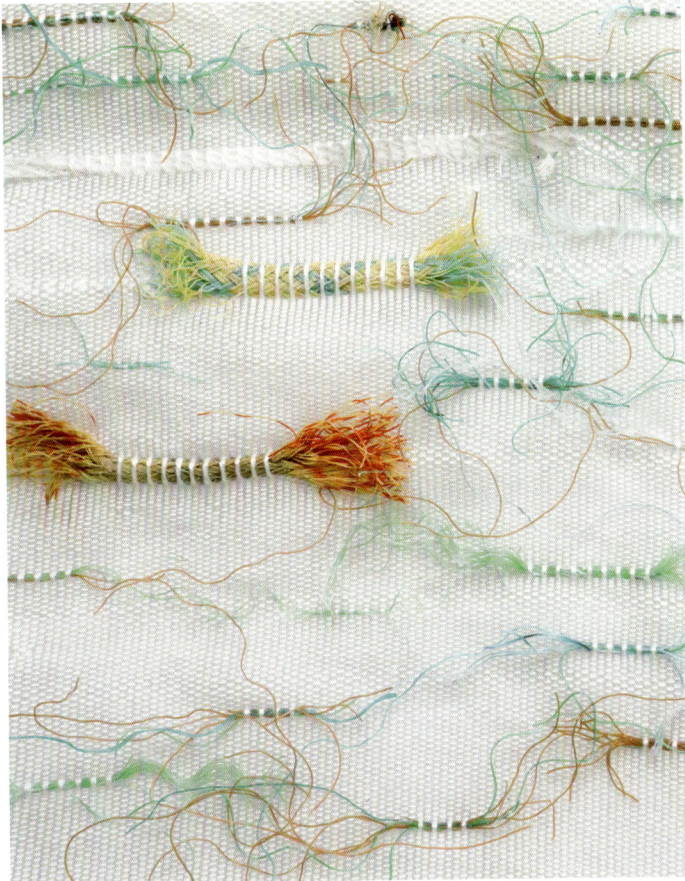

"I fell in love with textiles when I was a baby. I always had a blanket or cloth, and my mother tells me I was quite attached to them. This turned into an almost obsessive comfort habit of unraveling certain knots and playing with the threads—which I still do. In college I took a class focused on 'textiles as art.' We watched the documentary film Textile Magicians *[by Cristo Zañartu], which told the story of five different Japanese artists [Hiroyuki Shindo, Masakazu Kobayashi, Chiyoko Tanaka, Naomi Kobayashi, and Jun Tomita] working in harmony with nature, using textiles as their medium. This film blew my mind and my world right open. I changed majors after that, and textiles has been at the forefront of my career ever since."*

Dana Haim's childhood home in Miami, Florida, was filled with collected handmade relics and crafts, from which she still draws inspiration. Haim studied textile design (with a focus on weaving, silk-screening, and machine knitting) at the Rhode Island School of Design. After living and working briefly in Tel Aviv, she studied at London's Central Saint Martins. Her thesis project explored the preservation of craft in an increasingly digital age. Haim is Colombian American and has spent a lot of time in Latin America, observing and learning local practices, including natural dyeing, tapestry weaving, ceramics, and basketry. Recently she attended an artist residence at the Icelandic Textile Center in Blönduós, where she explored using repurposed fishing nets and lines foraged from seashores around the world.

OPPOSITE AND ABOVE
Hanging On for Dear Life series, 2023
Unraveled rope and repurposed fishing nets

Debra Sparrow

Vancouver, Canada

OPPOSITE
Woven blanket, 1991
Wool fiber, madder
root dye, tea dye;
66 × 61 inches
(168 × 155.5 cm)

ABOVE
Wall hanging, 2003
Wool fiber, madder
root dye, tea dye;
20 × 43 inches
(50 × 108 cm)

"In Salish country, we stand on our blankets. I will always be a weaver; I'm so honored to be a part of bringing Musqueam weaving back into the world. I asked my grandfather whether he remembered weaving and he said, 'Oh sure, I saw weaving. I used to watch my grandmother weave. She would sit in a shed with great big looms and other women. When I was four I would get into mischief playing with yarn. So they kicked me out of the shed. They were working on weaving for my naming ceremony.' He was eighty-three when he told me this. I said to him, 'You just connected me.' Now I had my identity to stand on, and that empowered me. Everything I did, I did for him. Now I'm teaching my daughter and my grandson. This is an exciting time; people are seeing value in being connected in your thread."

Debra Sparrow has been deeply involved in the revival of Musqueam weaving for more than thirty years: directly learning from the work of her ancestors. The Musqueam people are one of the three host nations of the Vancouver area. The Musqueam's ancestors, the Coast Salish, have lived in the Fraser River estuary (located in British Columbia's Lower Mainland) for thousands of years. Sparrow recognizes that weaving can offer stories of her heritage and also serve as a traditional form of education to effectively teach math, science, history, and philosophy. A desire to pass on the Salish weaving practice (and Musqueam history) to the future generations led to Sparrow's involvement in the cocreation of the Musqueam Museum School with the University of British Columbia.

Elise McMahon

Hudson, New York
b. 1986

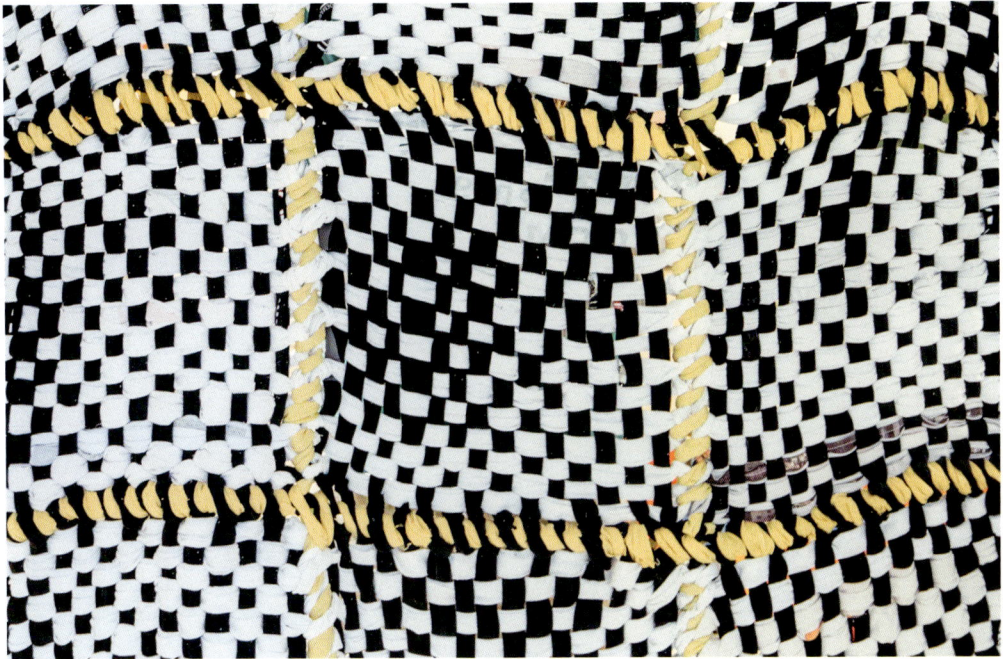

"My family always had sewing machines in the house for practical uses like mending, altering, and making simple things. I witnessed my mother, aunts, and grandmother care for their clothes and textiles in such a way that exudes care and slow consumption practices. We have shawls and kilts and blankets that have been in our family for over five generations. I see cloth as just one material I work with, but it is an incredible material. The cloth I use is obviously upcycled. I don't try to make it seem like 'virgin' material, because telling the story of our world's habits of consumption and waste is a priority for me. I love that working with cloth is very approachable as a craft. I host community mending and T-shirt weaving workshops. I find that people are emotionally uplifted as they learn new skills and realize they have the power to create their own daily objects."

As a child in Lake Forest, Illinois, Elise McMahon was taught to sew by her mother and grandmother. During her teenage years she learned garment pattern-making with help from a tutor, and found it empowering. McMahon studied furniture design at the Rhode Island School of Design and earned an MFA in Industrial Design (with a focus on waste and sustainability) at Parsons School of Design. She connected with upholstery as a core piece of her art practice and entered into a collaborative relationship with Renee Neblett of the Kokrobitey Institute in Ghana (which sources materials from one of the world's largest secondhand clothing markets). Neblett's practice of making clothing out of strictly secondhand fabrics influenced McMahon to focus her work on diverted materials from the American waste stream. She collaborated with textile artist and poet Francesca Capone to create T-shirt weaving looms, which are sold through McMahon's design studio, LikeMindedObjects, and are used in community workshops, with the aim of reducing textile waste shipped to other countries under the guise of recycling.

Federico Chávez Sosa and Dolores Santiago Arrellanas

Oaxaca, Mexico
b. 1959 (Federico), 1958 (Dolores)

Dolores: "I learned to dye and weave by my own will and with support from my parents. I really wanted to learn, even though it was rare for a woman to ask to learn because kitchen work is expected. My grandfather was a rug merchant and my father a rancher."

Federico: "I had the curiosity to learn to weave. I learned from my grandfather, father, and weavers of my community."

Master weavers and married couple Federico Chávez Sosa and Dolores Santiago Arrellanas are Indigenous Zapotec artists of Teotitlán del Valle. They skillfully adapt traditional designs with their own color combinations and patterns. Like thousands of weavers and dyers in the area, they were using aniline dyes, which yield bright colors but are irritating to the skin, eyes, and respiratory tract. They decided to return to the natural dyes used by their ancestors, including Sosa's grandfather. Their looms are built locally, with carved wood ratchets and wheels, and take about a month to complete. Along with their children, "Fe & Lola" operate a gallery, showroom, and workshop space under their aforementioned nicknames.

Isa Rodrigues

Brooklyn, New York, and Lagos, Portugal
b. 1978

OPPOSITE
Piscina, 2021 (detail)
Hand-painted cotton
warp, silk, cotton,
and linen weft;
44 × 33 inches
(112 × 84 cm)

ABOVE
Waves Studies, 2018
(detail)
Triple weave with
bamboo, linen,
and monofilament;
12 × 14 inches
(30 × 36 cm)

"When I was little, my grandmothers taught me embroidery, knitting, crocheting, and sewing—as a way of keeping my hands 'busy' but also because those were their crafts. My grandmothers were my first mentors. Textile work like lacemaking, palm leaf braiding, and weaving have a rich tradition in the South of Portugal, where I'm from, and it was an integral part of domestic and economic life until a few decades ago. Recently, I discovered that my great-great-grandmother was a weaver. No one in my family continued weaving after her, and in fact, there are very few weavers still practicing in the region where we are from. It makes me happy that I'm carrying on the craft."

Isa Rodrigues's love and curiosity for textiles started in her childhood home of Lagos, Portugal. She studied textile conservation in Lisbon, with a focus on understanding how textile materiality acts as an archive. Later, she joined the founding team of the Textile Arts Center in Brooklyn, a community-focused education project, and had the opportunity to expand her textile-making skills as an artist and artisan. Weaving, especially, resonated with Rodrigues because of the connection she felt to weavers throughout history. She experienced weaving as a feeling of homecoming. Teaching has also been central to her relationship with cloth. The Textile Arts Center was born from the vision of creating a shared space for co-learning and experimenting (a reflection of how textile techniques have been traditionally practiced and taught). Rodrigues sees teaching as a way to preserve textile material culture, through craft education and sharing the stories contained within.

James Bassler

Palm Springs, California
b. 1933

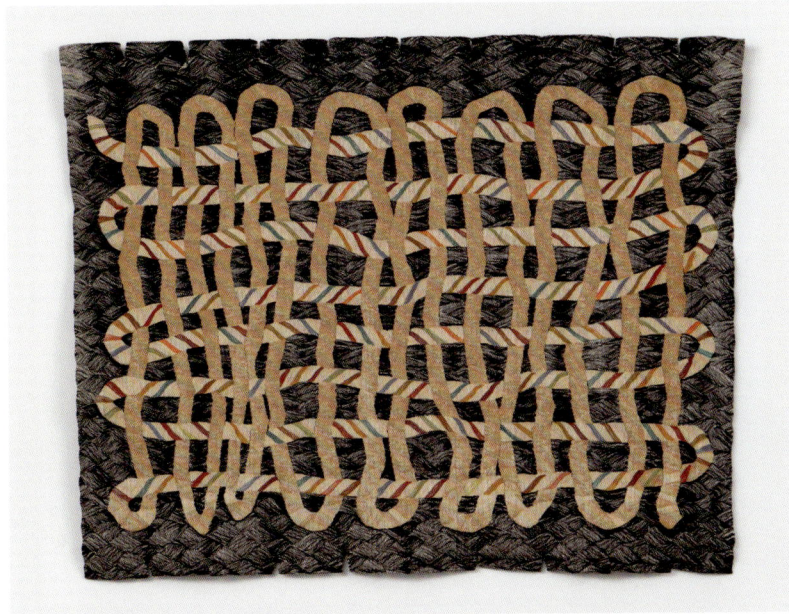

OPPOSITE
On Inca Time, 2019
Scaffold weave, with wool, silk, linen, ramie, sisal, and cotton
Natural and synthetic dyes;
43 × 36¾ inches
(109 × 93 cm)

ABOVE
Weaving with Coyuche, 2016
Linen warp, wedge weave
Natural brown cotton from Oaxaca (coyuche), black embroidery floss, and silk;
33½ × 42 inches
(85 × 107 cm)

"*My father was a professional major league baseball player. However, his other interests included making hooked rugs. He was a Mennonite, brought up in Lancaster, Pennsylvania. Mennonites are diligent workers. He hooked rugs in the wintertime, when it wasn't baseball season. He used my mother's stockings. The dyeing process consisted of pots on the stove. That was my introduction to fiber arts. At his end of life, I got him hooking rugs again.*"

James Bassler was born in Santa Monica, California. He began college studies at the University of California, Los Angeles (UCLA), before being drafted to Germany. There, he observed the ability of people to start their lives over after devastation. Following his service in the army, Bassler bought a passenger ticket to Hong Kong and then traveled throughout India and Indonesia. These travels in Asia during the 1950s introduced him to weaving as an integral part of daily life. He returned to UCLA and began making work in the small weaving department taught by Bernard Kester. Later, Bassler and his wife, Veralee, visited Oaxaca, Mexico, and were enthralled by the indigenous weaving community. The Basslers lived and taught in Oaxaca for many years. In the 1980s, while researching Navajo weaving, Bassler came across a series of distinctive blankets woven in a diagonal construction called "wedge weaving." This inspired him to take a more conceptual approach to his work. Over the years Bassler has continued to incorporate techniques from various ancient cultures into his artistic process, an interest which he attributes to his enduring desire to find an alternative to the pace of modern society. Bassler is a professor emeritus in the department of Design Media Arts at UCLA.

Jovencio de la Paz

Eugene, Oregon
b. 1986

OPPOSITE
Bionumeric Organisms, 2019
Woven using Tronrud
TC2 loom

LEFT
Didderen
Woven using Tronrud
TC2 loom

"Cloth and textiles are the vantage point from which I view the past, present, and future. As a student of weaving, I attempt to study human history through the pervasive narrative of cloth: From the advent of agriculture to the epoch of global colonialism, from the industrial revolution to the punch-card loom and early computer technology, weaving is an essential commodity and mechanical knowledge that has influenced the development of human history. This is a personal exploration for me, as an immigrant child and the cultural product of European conquest in Southeast Asia. My relationship with cloth is one of attempting to locate my personal narrative within these larger narratives.

"In the last couple of years, I taught my mother and grandmother how to weave on a floor loom, which I always think is a funny reversal of how we generally characterize the passing of this kind of knowledge.

A native of Singapore, Jovencio de la Paz became a citizen of the United States in 1994. Their current work, with textiles and fiber processes, explores the intersecting histories of weaving and modern computers. Meeting across millennia, the stories of weaving and computation unfold as a space of speculation. Trained in traditional processes of weaving, dyeing, and stitchwork but reveling in the complexities and contradictions of digital culture, they work to find relationships between concerns of language, embodiment, pattern, and code and broad concerns of ancient technology, speculative futures, and the phenomenon of emergence. Currently, de la Paz is an associate professor and curricular head of Fibers at the University of Oregon.

Kelly Harris Smith

Boston, Massachusetts
b. 1979

"My grandmother inspired me throughout my journey in textiles. She worked in a Levi Strauss factory in the 1950s and in a button factory. She was always making things with her hands: mending clothing, quilting and drapery, needlepoint embroidery, cross-stitch, and crochet. Seeing everything she made and hearing stories about the creativity she had inspired me to try to sew and experiment with textiles myself."

Born in Virginia, Kelly Harris Smith received her first sewing machine in second grade and started making outfits for her dolls. While in college studying abroad in Florence, she was exposed to Italian furniture and design shops and the Salone furniture fair in Milan, which opened her eyes and mind to the world of textiles. After graduation, Harris Smith worked in architecture and continued sewing on the weekends, particularly with felt. She began sourcing higher-quality wool felt from a mill in Germany. This relationship grew when the mill asked if she wanted to distribute their felt in North America, which led to the cofounding of FilzFelt with business partner Traci Roloff (acquired by Knoll, Inc., in 2011). Now Harris Smith works as a designer and creative director for her eponymous brand specializing in natural, sustainable, and recycled materials. Her fabrics are made with postconsumer recycled polyester (primarily from PET water bottles) and are woven in family- and employee-owned mills in the United States and Canada. Harris Smith is also the founder of Minni, a community creative space in Boston offering art and design education to young children.

Marina Contro

San Francisco, California
b. 1987

OPPOSITE
Untitled II, 2016
Photographed
handwoven cotton

ABOVE
Woven hemp and
cotton, turned twill
blocks

"Many of the women in my family are artists and have a keen sense for design, travel, and fashion. I feel that connection between my work and them when I am in my studio. It's powerful to build upon the legacy of my grandmother, Mary Anne, and my aunt, Antonia, who have really encouraged me to go deeper into my work, to take it seriously, and to be courageous."

"I'm very aware of cloth; I think about it all the time. We are all touching cloth for most of the day. We're clothed in it, we dry ourselves with it, we sleep on it."

Marina Contro was born in Chicago, Illinois, and received a BA in Religious Studies from University of Colorado Boulder and an MFA in Fiber from Cranbrook Academy of Art in 2017. She is deeply interested in material, technique, and the relationship between art and craft. Contro uses an antique loom built in Vermont in the late nineteenth century. Her art plays with function, challenging the way in which we interact with the objects around us. She feels that even using a dish towel can be a special experience if we stay open to certain beauties. Over the past decade, Contro has forged relationships with fiber producers across the United States. She loves to understand their different methods and the land that produces these products. Contro is a professor in the Textiles program at California College of the Arts.

Michelle Yi Martin

San Francisco, California
b. 1977

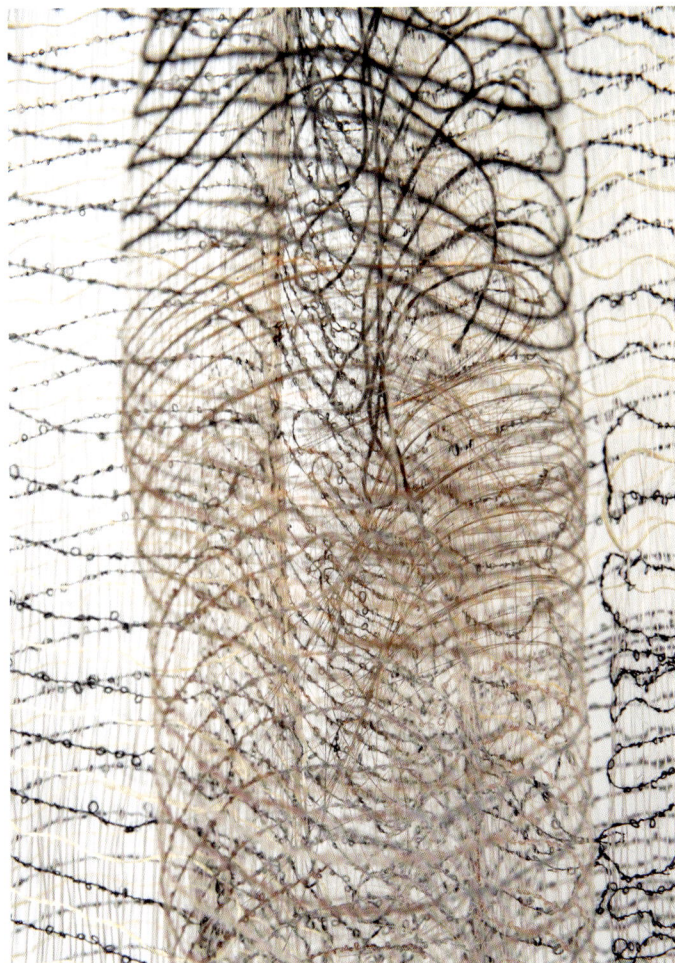

In 2017, Michelle and I attended an artist residency together in Blönduós, Iceland. We landed in Reykjavik and sought out hot springs to dip into, then traveled north by bus. Michelle was primarily working in sewn pieces then—using fabric from her grandmother's Korean hanbok dresses. At the Icelandic Textile Center we had access to a beautiful weaving studio on the top floor of a former women's dormitory. Michelle took advantage of this time to experiment on the many floor looms.

—Lena

OPPOSITE
Nightjars, 2023
Cotton, wool, linen, and paper;
31 × 30½ inches, framed (79 × 78 cm)

ABOVE
Roost Mate, 2024
Copper, horsehair, monofilament, silk, wool
75 × 32 inches (190 × 81 cm)

"My relationship with textiles is that of awe, most closely in the religious sense. I find instantaneous fulfillment in the connection made to a practice that has allowed human civilization to thrive. I often wonder if my ancestors held the same fibers in their hands as I do, or if they also saw the face of the cosmos in their weavings. There is such deep wisdom from deep time.

"My grandmother taught me how to make fine stitches, bojagi, for traditional quilts and other textiles. The cloth often came from old hanboks, which are Korean folk attire made of ramie and silk. They were then pieced together with worn American-made denim and cotton—such a metaphor of her journey. She never let anything go to waste, and I can still feel what it was like to sit next to her in complete silence, listening as her time-defined fingers made the finest stitches."

Michelle Yi Martin is a multidisciplinary artist and weaver, born in Seoul, South Korea. At age two she immigrated, with her family, to San Francisco. Yi Martin earned a BA from Santa Clara University in California and an MA from the University of San Francisco, where she became active in the Teaching for Excellence and Social Justice program. She has been an educator of the humanities, interdisciplinary art, and progressive education for more than twenty years. Her art practice developed in this intersection of history, human engagement, craft, experimentation, and fine art. As a Korean American immigrant woman, she lives in the "in-between" space where the threads of her identity converge. Her practice and choice of materials is an expression where conventional language is limited. While she honors the ancient language of fiber, Yi Martin also makes space for other mediums to join the conversation: light, ink, sound, and movement.

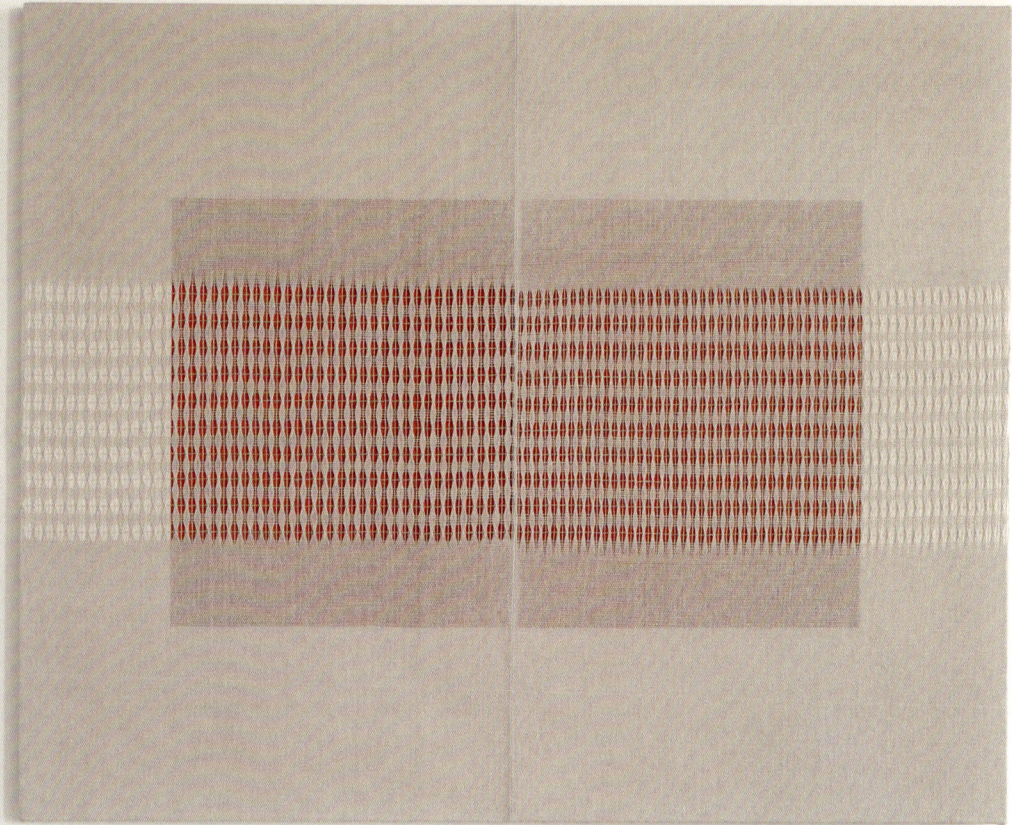

Rachel DuVall

Los Angeles, California
b. 1986

OPPOSITE
Madder Flashe Lace,
2021
Woven linen, flashe
paint; 48 × 60 inches
(122 × 152 cm)

ABOVE
Woven linen (detail)

"Weaving is a detailed process with lots of measuring, counting, and repetition. Through this repetition, I can live in the moment and get lost in the building up of the fabric line by line. As a mother of two small children, I appreciate my time at the loom even more as a place of calm and something that I cannot wait to share with them as they grow older. There is such joy in bringing my daughter to the studio and giving her yarn to see what she makes."

Rachel DuVall was born in West Grove, Pennsylvania. Her interest in textiles came from her mother, who generally enjoyed making things from scratch: spinning fiber, crocheting, and making soap and cheese from the dairy goats they raised. In 2008, DuVall received a BFA in Fiber from the Maryland Institute College of Art. When she was in school, DuVall didn't intend to work with fiber. However, after taking a class spent working on a floor loom, she was hooked. It was the meditative practice behind weaving that felt most compelling. She enjoys the balance between the inherent softness of a textile and its measured beginnings. Her residency at the Josef & Anni Albers Foundation in early 2020 broadened her artistic horizons, allowing her to take a break from her regular work and try new techniques such as going more in depth with optical mixing and combining painting with weaving.

Rachel Meginnes

Bakersville, North Carolina
b. 1977

"First and foremost, I was encouraged to work with cloth by my immediate family. In high school, a best friend of mine suggested I learn how to weave. It was her suggestion that pointed me down this path that I have remained on ever since. [As an undergraduate,] I studied traditional textile techniques (hand-dyeing and weaving on the floor loom). After school, I studied sakiori and ikat techniques in Japan and apprenticed as a rug weaver in DownEast Maine, where I gained skills in natural dyeing and shaft-switch rug weaving. In graduate school, I expanded my interest in textiles to include the deconstruction of woven structures and explored the meaning that materials can hold."

Rachel Meginnes was raised in rural Vermont, and she grew up surrounded by hooked rugs made by her mother and grandmother. Cut from recycled wool cloth, these works hung on the walls (and laid on the floors) of her childhood home. From a young age, her eye was trained to see the potential in discarded materials. Meginnes's current practice revolves around the act of repurposing through her own collection and through the deconstruction

and reutilization of vintage textiles. Rachel studied at Earlham College and the University of Washington. Outside of school, she expanded her knowledge of textiles in India, New Zealand, and Japan. Meginnes has taught in formal academic settings, craft contexts, prison workshops, and after-school programs. She has guided artists through growth and challenge, offering them insight, clarity, and the momentum they need to move forward.

Rachel Snack

Philadelphia, Pennsylvania
b. 1990

"My grandfather worked in a fabric-dyeing mill in Paterson, New Jersey, and my great-great-grandmother worked in a weaving mill at some point in her life, although I don't have many details. Both of these jobs were unglamorous and out of necessity.

"I started weaving while obtaining my undergraduate degree. I began my education by painting and making ceramics; however, when I later enrolled in an introduction to textiles class, there was a kinship I felt the first time I attempted to weave cloth. I saw weaving as a tangible way to memorialize 'place' (sacred space), by creating a dialect between maker and loom."

Rachel Snack was artistic and creative from a young age, growing up in New Jersey. Her mother, an occasional quilter, has been her biggest supporter of her artistic interests. Snack studied fiber and material at the Art Institute of Chicago, and textile design at Philadelphia University. She is the founder of Weaver House, a textile studio, yarn shop, and weaving school dedicated to preserving craft tradition through handmaking and weaving education. Workshops at Weaver House include all levels of weaving, as well as other experimental techniques within fiber art and sculpture. When she is weaving, Snack feels as if the loom is an extension of herself, and that she is connected to other weavers who have come before her—a part of a collective strand. Snack has been an artist-in-residence in Mexico, Ireland, and Peru.

Rhiannon Griego

Santa Fe, New Mexico
b. 1982

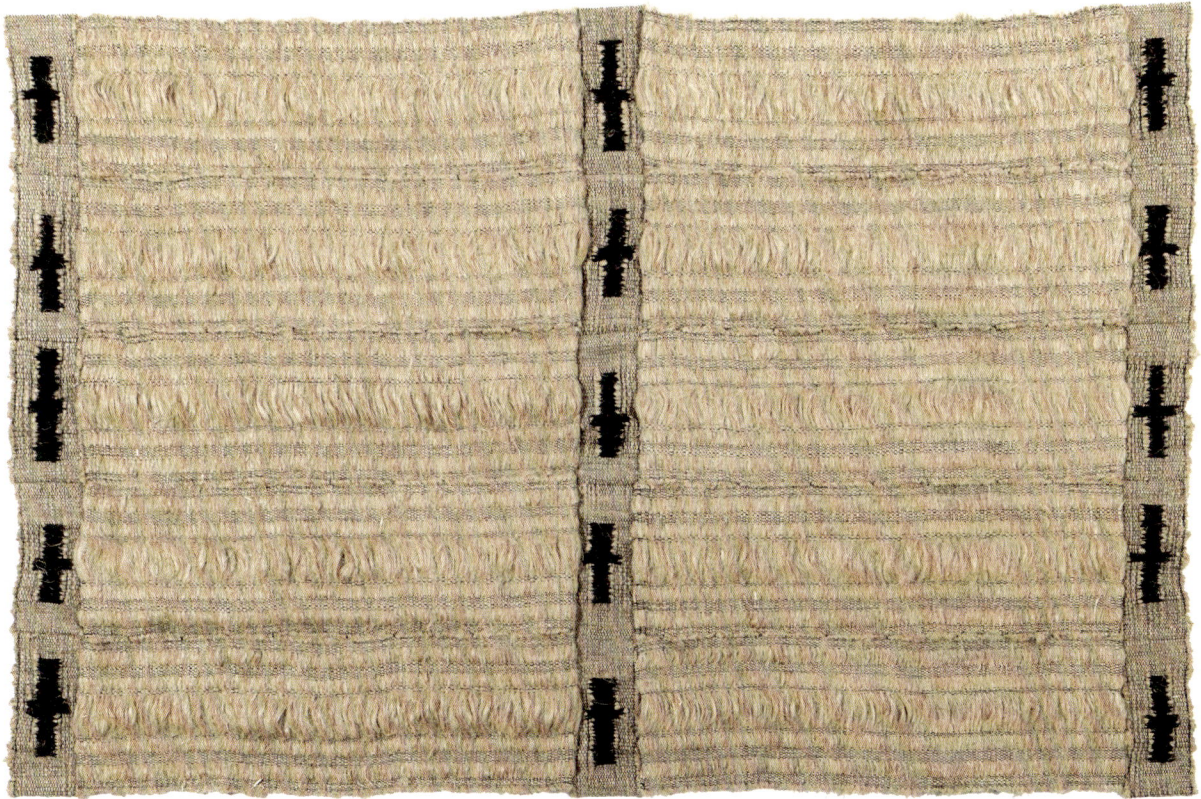

OPPOSITE
The Wall, 2020
Raw hemp
and cotton;
105 × 80 inches
(267 × 203 cm)

ABOVE
Four Directions, 2020
Raw hemp, cotton,
and wool;
45 × 72½ inches
(114 × 118 cm)

"My objective with my wearable artwork is to reinvigorate daily interaction with cloth and transform the persona [of the wearer]. Our modern society is so used to machine-made, mass-produced garments that many can't identify what type of fiber is worn, or remember how interwoven we are with Earth."

Raised in California, Rhiannon Griego is deeply connected to her Mexican, Tohono O'odham, and Spanish heritage. Both of her grandmothers crocheted, and her father's family in New Mexico practiced weaving and dyeing. In her early twenties she began to paint and do beadwork. Since 2012, Griego has studied and practiced the philosophies of Saori Zen weaving, a contemporary handweaving method founded by Japanese artist Misao Jo. The wabi sabi nature of Saori Zen weaving has moved her to create dimensional landscapes and embrace the beauty of imperfection within her textiles. Her work embodies the spirit of the land and the deserts of the American Southwest. Griego's heritage provides artistic portals through which she feels a connection with her ancestors. She has a strong reverence for the relationship between humans and the earth's land and soil, and uses plants in her work for medicinal and dye material.

Sheila Hicks

Paris, France, and Manhattan, New York
b. 1934

OPPOSITE
Settled Solidly, 2017
Silk; 10 × 8¼ inches
(25 × 21 cm)

RIGHT
RDCL, 2014
Linen and cotton;
8 × 11½ inches
(20 × 29 cm)

"I move from idea to finished work acrobatically—it's as though I can feel the clouds shifting and the light coming and going. But because I frequently use fiber and textiles, I'm also quite specific in the way I work; unlike a video artist or a digital artist, I'm physically engaged in the creation of all my work. It's a manual practice but filtered through the optics of architecture, photography, form, material, and color. A couple of years ago, I received an honorary doctorate from my school—I went to Yale in the fifties—and it made me very happy because it validated my choice to work and live as an artist. It meant that I could contribute something to the other fields, and so I'm seeking out what that might be, unlike many artists, who are seeking simply to express themselves."

Sheila Hicks spent much of her childhood on the road as her father followed opportunities for paid work. This migratory existence, as she has described it, came to define her career as an artist, working and traveling around the world. She sees textiles as universal, crucial, and essential in all cultures. In the late fifties, she received a Fulbright scholarship to paint in Chile. While in South America she developed her interest in working with fibers.

Hicks has traveled through five continents, studying the local culture in Mexico, France, Morocco, India, Chile, Sweden, Israel, Saudi Arabia, Japan, and South Africa. She has developed relationships with designers, artisans, industrialists, architects, politicians, and cultural leaders worldwide. Her work varies in scale from small handwoven pieces to large sculptural piles. She now divides her time between her Paris studio and New York.

Susana Vicente Galan

Oaxaca, Mexico
b. 1979

OPPOSITE
Cortina Maguey, 2024
Woven handmade
thread from maguey
(agave) plant;
1 cm grid pattern

ABOVE
Detail

"Weaving is what we do here in Teotitlán del Valle. My father taught me, starting with what we call the "greca," a geometric shape mimicking the ruins of Monte Albán (the archaeological site of the Mesoamerican city). When young people here start learning to weave, they usually start with this technique because it's like math, counting stitches to create patterns. It helps us learn faster, as my father used to say. The 'greca' symbolizes the stages of our life because it has four steps: birth, growth, reproduction, and death. It represents our entire life's journey. All of my children learned to weave when they were very young."

Susana Vicente Galan weaves in her home workshop in Teotitlán del Valle, Oaxaca. She learned to weave on a treadle loom when she was eight years old, and she continues a long family tradition of weaving in Teotitlán. For her collaboration with Twenty One Tonnes and Hermano Maguey, Vicente Galan weaves with leaves of the maguey (agave) plant, utilizing the leftover leaves from mezcal production. Twenty One Tonnes is the design studio of Chessa Osburn and Mary Jane Bolton. Based in Los Angeles, they produce thoughtfully crafted pieces for interiors in collaboration with artisan partners in Ghana, Mexico, Japan, and Colombia. Hermano Maguey is a Oaxaca-based project focused on community development around the maguey-mezcal ecosystem. Prior to Vicente Galan threading the maguey fibers on her treadle loom, the leaves are pressed, whipped, combed, and finally twisted into lengths of slender cord. The result of this labor-intensive craft process is woven cloth that is delicate yet strong, and each piece celebrates the material it is made from. Vicente Galan is also an expert dyer, using materials like black sapote fruit, cochineal, and indigo.

Susie Taylor

Rochester, New York
b. 1967

"When I was growing up in a large family, hand-me-downs were a necessity. My mother, a master of thrift, patched and mended our clothes, making them last long past their prime. As a child, I really didn't think of cloth as anything but utilitarian. That changed when I started accompanying my mom to the fabric store, where I saw aisles of woven and printed fabric bolts.

"Early in my education, I remember thinking how profound it was to be able to make cloth. Weaving and textiles are how I interact with and make sense of the world around me, and I especially love the international camaraderie that I have with so many brilliant weavers worldwide. It certainly feels like I am doing what I was meant to do, and I feel strongly about contributing something to the broader tradition of weaving."

Susie Taylor was born in Fort Collins, Colorado, and as a young adult, her awareness of weaving was an awakening she compares to finding a missing puzzle piece. Taylor received her BFA from the Kansas City Art Institute and her MFA from the University of California, Los Angeles. Her work explores geometric abstraction through the tradition of weaving, a process that requires a creative and technical mindset to solve visual and structural puzzles. Imagery, rendered by the interlacing of warp and weft, is embedded in the very structure of the cloth. Inspired by formalism and the Bauhaus, her compositions include basic shapes like blocks and stripes to address pattern, symmetry, and color interaction, as well as the notion that ordered systems can still flirt with chance, interruption, and improvisation. She has studied and worked, and continues to create, within the lineage of the Bauhaus and Black Mountain College weavers.

OPPOSITE
Social Fabric, 2022
Woven cotton; 88 × 75 inches
(224 × 190 cm)

ABOVE
Iconic Stripes 4, 2022
Woven cotton; 44 × 33 inches
(112 × 84 cm)

Travis Meinolf

Lagunitas, California
b. 1978

I met with Travis twice to talk about his work and photograph him for the book, first at his weaving school in San Anselmo, a fifteen-mile drive from my house. Travis is a generous multitasker: He waved in small kids walking down the street and played a song on his accordion, while touring me around his school and helping community weavers on their looms as needed. The second time we met was at the Eames Institute in Petaluma, the property of legendary industrial designers Charles and Ray Eames, where he is growing their weaving studio.

—Lena

OPPOSITE AND LEFT
Woven blankets
Cotton and wool

"I was studying industrial design at San Francisco State University, but making things, like weaving, where I get to be mostly responsible for the labor that is involved, and building that thread by thread, felt nourishing. I completed my design degree, but I always kept weaving as a practice. I went to California College of the Arts and got a textiles degree so I could figure out where I could find the intersection of the practice and the culture at large."

Travis Meinolf is the founder of the Meinolf Weaving School in San Anselmo, California—located near the elementary school Meinolf attended as a child. The weaving school is a continuation of his lifelong project of connecting to people via new relationships to the process of weaving. Travis earned a bachelor's degree in Industrial Design from San Francisco State University and a master's degree in Fine Art from the California College of the Arts. Prior to establishing a weaving school, most of his teaching was done in public spaces like parks, streets, subways, and libraries alongside more traditional locations like schools, museums, and universities. By weaving in public, and having discussions with the public about their connections to textiles, Meinolf has learned about the ways textiles affect people in their lives. He finds weaving to be a way to offer comfortable socializing; it opens doors for people to interact that otherwise might feel a little awkward.

Recycled Jersey Weaving

Many people are familiar with the small peg looms used in potholder weaving kits. For a long time, I have wanted to make an extra-large custom peg loom. Elise McMahon (page 33) leads community-focused workshops using textile waste with large peg looms she has designed and manufactured. Since making my own peg loom, I have enjoyed weaving a handful of floor mats using discarded T-shirts. Artists, craftspeople, and homemakers have always utilized scrap waste for projects—creating rag rugs, quilts, and more. *Basahan*, a Tagalog word for rags, describes weavings made of jersey scraps, used commonly as potholders and doormats in the Philippines.

MATERIALS

2 wooden deck balusters, 2 × 2 × 36 inches (5 × 5 × 91 cm)

2 wooden deck balusters, 2 × 2 × 29½ inches (5 × 5 × 75 cm)

Pencil

Ruler

Hammer

1 box ¾-inch (2 cm) nails (quantity: 182)

Four 3-inch (7.5 cm) wood screws and electric screwdriver

3–4 Large and Extra Large T-shirts

4–5 Small and Medium T-shirts

Scissors

illustration A

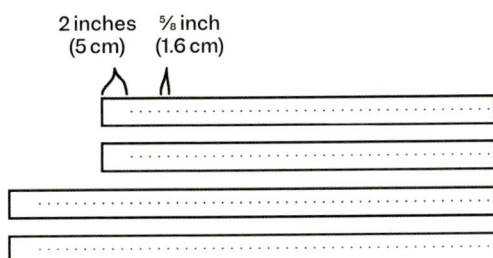

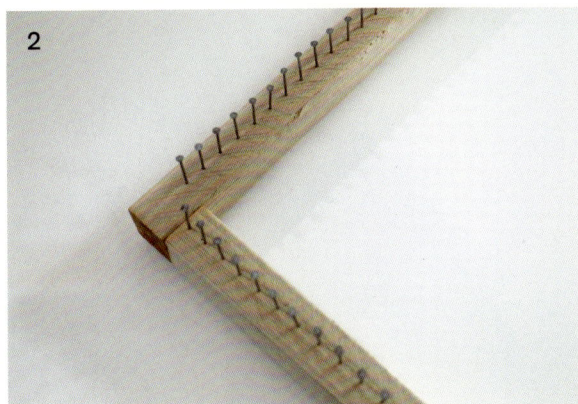

illustration B

2 inches (5 cm)   ⅝ inch (1.6 cm)

NOTE: *Start saving old T-shirts, and shop at charity stores to find inexpensive tees. T-shirts can be 100 percent cotton or a blend of cotton and synthetic yarn. Men's T-shirts work best because of their boxy shape (avoid using tees with contoured sides). In creating the loom, my kids did the nailing for me.*

INSTRUCTIONS

1. Dot the balusters with pencil marks, as shown in illustration A. The first pencil mark begins 2 inches (5 cm) from the end, followed by a mark every ⅝ inch (1.6 cm) with a total of 40 marks on the shorter balusters and 50 marks on the longer balusters. Hammer a nail (approximately ½ inch [1.3 cm] deep) at each pencil mark. The nails do not need to be perfectly straight.

2. Connect the balusters into a rectangular frame, using a screwdriver and screw in each corner, as shown in illustration B. The frame should feel sturdy and rigid.

   After a year of use, my frame lost some strength, and I reinforced each corner from the back by screwing on 4 x 4-inch (10 x 10 cm) squares of plywood.

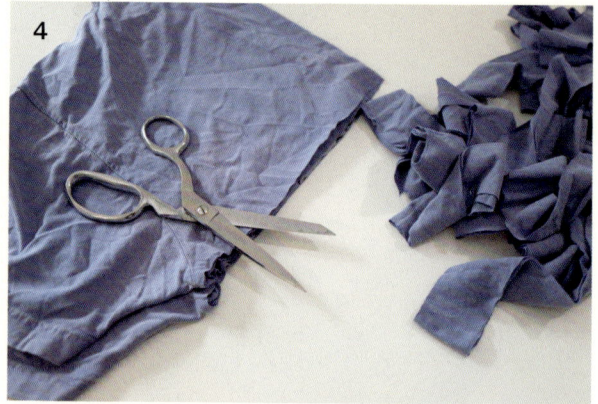

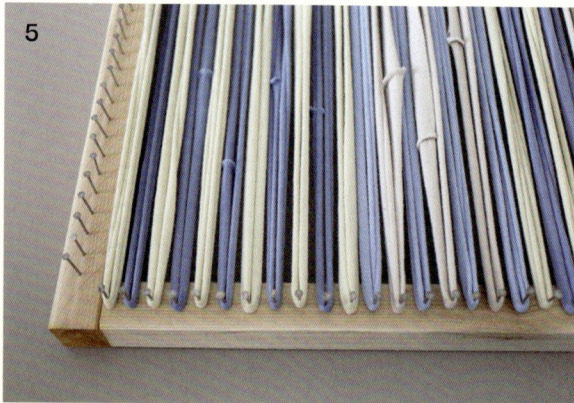

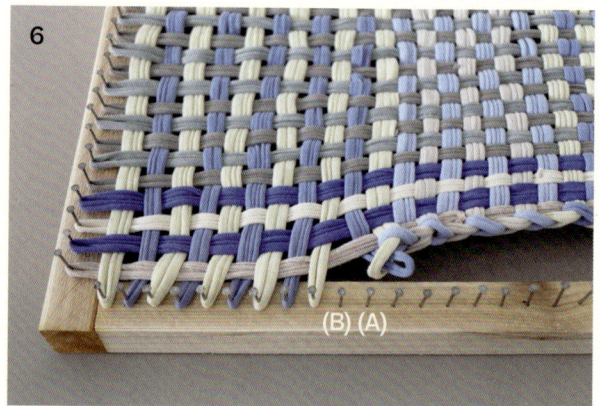

(B) (A)

3. Lay a T-shirt flat and fold it in half lengthwise.
    Cut off the bottom hem and place the hem in a
    discard pile.

4. Cut a strip of fabric by eye, 1½–2 inches
    (4–5 cm) in width (measuring is not necessary).
    Continue cutting strips up to the underarm of
    the tee. Repeat with all T-shirts. Take unused
    scraps (including the hem) to a textile recycling
    program.

5. Beginning with the longer loops, stretch one
    loop across the loom at a time until all of the
    nails are used. With the longer stretched loops
    facing vertically, take a shorter loop and carry
    it under and over each vertical loop—from nail
    to nail. Continue for all of the nails.

6. To remove the weaving from the loom, start in
    one corner and remove a single loop (A) from
    a nail. Moving clockwise, carefully remove the
    adjacent loop (B) and pull loop B through loop
    A. Drop loop A. Continue this motion, moving
    around the entire perimeter of the loom.
    Take the last loop and tuck it deep into the
    woven mat.

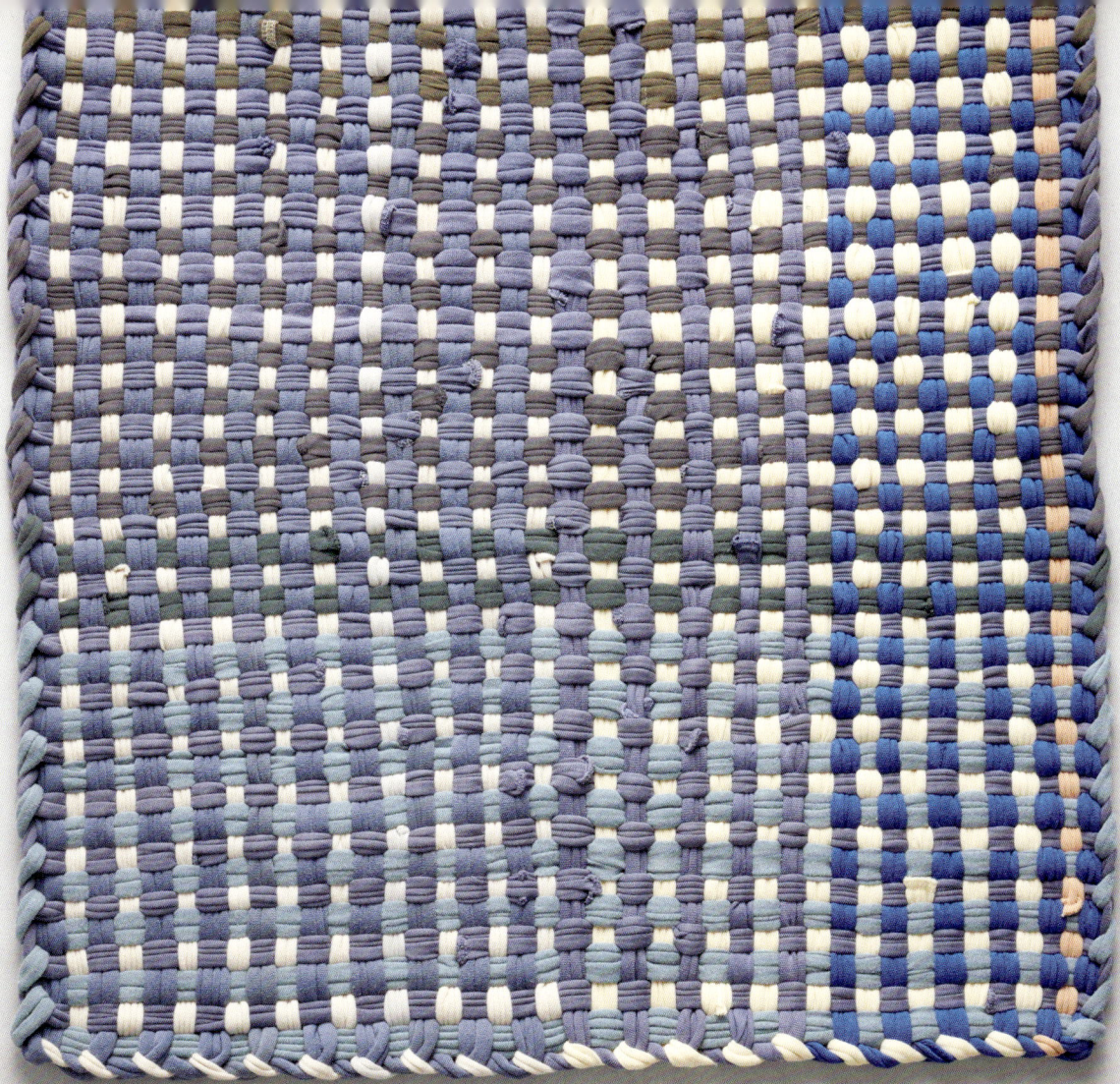

Nature Weaving & Braiding

I learned to weave a pine needle basket at age nine, and I continued with a practice of weaving and braiding collected nature—things like seaweed, grasses, and soft twigs. When my own kids were little, and my pace slowed to theirs, weaving with found nature remained an accessible creative outlet. While researching for this book, I began to see my habit through a larger lens. In *Braiding Sweetgrass*, author Robin Wall Kimmerer writes about the literal hands-on tradition of tending to and braiding grass, and the metaphorical braiding of an intertwining spirit and story. I think about the Native Ohlone and Miwok people who lived in my home of Northern California—whose traditional handwork was taught to me when I wove my first pine needle basket, and whose spirit is alive in their woven and braided work still intact today.

MATERIALS

Collected natural materials, approximately 18–30 pieces

2 rubber bands

2 twist ties

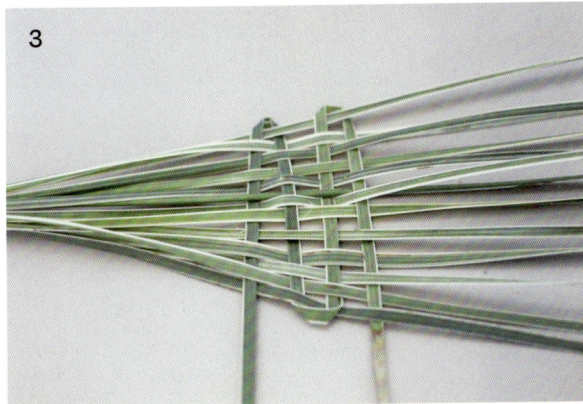

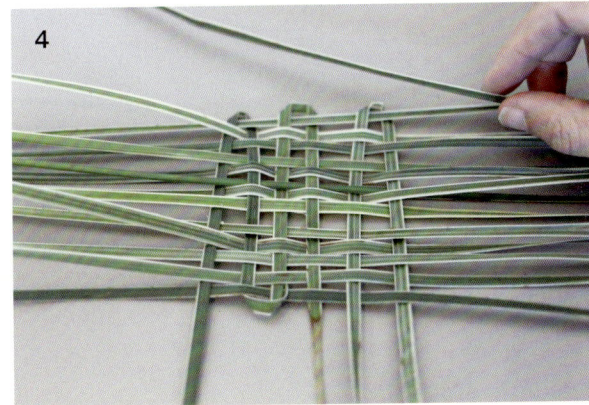

NOTE: *This project is meant to be an experimental practice. Look around in your environment for natural materials that share qualities with yarn and cloth—they should be pliable and long and narrow in shape. For braiding, I bundle the material with a rubber band at one end and create a simple three-strand braid. I finish the braid by binding the ends with the same braid material. For weaving, follow the instructions below.*

INSTRUCTIONS

1. Take approximately twelve pieces of found material and secure one end with a rubber band or twist tie, to create the warp. Pick up a new piece of the material to use as the weft. Several inches below the band, begin weaving by passing the weft over/under the warp strands. At the end of the warp, manipulate the weft material to turn back and weave a second row, now going under/over.

2+3. Continue weaving back and forth with the weft strand.

4. When a weft strand ends, the last inch can be either left hanging off or woven back into the warp. As the weaving progresses, untie the rubber band or twist tie, and allow the warp to release into parallel rows. End the weaving simply by stopping when desired.

Sew and Quilt

Pulling Thread

SEWING is the process of attaching materials using stitches made with a sewing needle and thread. Some basic hand-sewing stitches include the running stitch, slip stitch, backstitch, and overcast stitch. The running stitch is the simplest, and it is usually done three or four stitches at a time. A slip stitch is not visible externally because the needle passes inside the folded edges of fabric. A backstitch is made by sewing one stitch length backward on the front side, and two stitch lengths forward on the reverse side (to form a solid line of stitching on both sides). An overcast stitch is used to enclose an unfinished edge of cloth to prevent fraying. Approximately a dozen more basic hand and machine stitches are traditionally used.

Sewing Traditions

More than twenty thousand years ago, humans of the Stone Age joined pieces of material like animal skins using bone and horn needles and animal sinew for thread. The Inuit people of northern Canada, Greenland, and Alaska used tendons from caribou for thread with needles made of bone. The Indigenous people of the American plains and Canadian prairies used similar methods. Zulu tribespeople in Africa used thin strips of palm leaf as thread to stitch wider strips of palm leaves together. Around the fourteenth century, iron needles were invented, and later sewing needles were made of steel (which is still used today).

The sewing practice of tatreez originated in Palestine in the Canaanite era (three thousand years ago). Tatreez uses colored threads and the fallahi stitch (cross-stitch). Pojagi (also referred to as bojagi) is the ancient Korean folk tradition of sewing textiles for both everyday and ceremonial use. Jogakbo (or chogakpo) means "small segments" in Korean and is the style of patchwork used to create pojagi from scraps of leftover fabrics. Niki Tsukamoto's (page 109) commission work includes large jogakbo pojagi curtains, using lightweight fabric to allow sunlight to filter through. Adam Pogue (page 75) and Kiva Motnyk (page 95) also work with pojagi techniques.

Boro is a Japanese method of sewing cloth remnants, developed out of practical necessity in the Edo period (1603–1867). The name is a shortening of boroboro, meaning "something tattered or repaired." Usually made with cotton, linen, and hemp fabric, boro textiles are handwoven and stitched together to create a multilayered material, traditionally used for warm clothing.

Mola, or molas, is a sewing method developed by Indigenous Guna people from Panama and Colombia around the 1850s. Molas are made using a reverse appliqué technique where several layers of colored cloth (usually cotton) are sewn together, and the design (often flowers, birds, reptiles, and other animals and emblems of nature) is then formed by cutting away parts of each layer. Using a similar method, Hmong people in Laos are known for a reverse appliqué called *paj ntaub*, meaning "flower cloth" and "story cloth," that depicts life events.

Sewing changed significantly when European and American inventors began to successfully make simple sewing machines that mimicked hand-sewing. In 1846, Elias Howe of Massachusetts patented his sewing machine, dramatically changing the way clothing was manufactured. In 1851, New Yorker Isaac M. Singer invented a sewing machine with an overhanging arm, making it possible to sew on any part of the garment. Singer also patented the foot treadle and the spring-equipped presser foot (used for holding down the fabric while sewing). By 1870, the sewing machine was capable of making six hundred stitches per minute (while an experienced hand-sewer could make twenty-five stitches in the same period of time).

QUILTING involves sewing two layers of fabric with a layer of padding in between, held together by lines of stitching. Quilting makes use of smaller pieces of cloth, with the quilt top typically being the most detailed portion of a finished piece. The origin of the word "quilt" comes from the Latin word *culcita*, meaning "a stuffed mattress or cushion." Originally a utilitarian item, quilts are also a canvas for cultural and self-expression.

Quilting Traditions

Quilting can be traced back to the Middle Ages in Europe. The Victoria and Albert Museum in England has some of the earliest examples of quilting from Europe and Asia. Ralli quilts from Pakistan's Sindh province are known for their diagonal placement of blocks of dyed cloth. Thick thread stitches are made in straight lines, sewing together the designed layer with the bottom layer of old shawls or similar material. Bargello quilts from Italy and Hungary were inspired by needlepoint designs. Kantha quilts in Bangladesh are made by repurposing worn-out saris or sarongs in whole pieces sewn together with a running stitch for a rippling effect. *Kantha*—a word believed to be derived from the Sanskrit word *kontha*, meaning "rags"—means "patched cloth" and refers to both the style of quilting and the stitch itself (a small, straight running stitch).

Hawaiian quilts traditionally use botanical patterns, made from a single big piece of cloth with a cut layer of fabric on top, typically pairing a vibrant tone with white. Pat Gorelangton (page 111) learned traditional Hawaiian quilting from her mentor John Serrao. Off the coast of Newfoundland in eastern Canada, Fogo Island quilters carry on a long tradition of patchwork quilting, using and reusing colorful, patterned fabric.

When European colonists settled in the United States, scrap cloth was used for making quilted bed coverings because textiles were scarce. Enslaved women sewed quilts from scraps on the plantations in which they lived, including the women of the Pettway Plantation in Gee's Bend, Alabama. Doris Pettway Mosely (85) and Sharon Pettway Williams (121) continue this heritage art form, creating quilted cloth as their ancestors did before them.

Adam Pogue

Los Angeles, California
b. 1978

"I tried a sculpture course at my local college, and I realized I could create interesting shapes and volume by sewing material together and stuffing it with batting. I made a few small soft sculptures out of old clothes and stuff from the thrift store. It was just a needle, thread, and fabrics. I made other things for myself here and there, and then a lightbulb went on—this is what I could offer others. This is what I want to do with my life. It was a self-discovery."

Adam Pogue wanted to be an architect as a child. Born in Tacoma, Washington, he lived briefly in Utah and then spent the majority of his childhood in Southern California. He spent time drawing floor plans and elevations. He took architecture courses in college, with hopes of attending the Southern California Institute of Architecture. Without the means to make it happen, he realized he could put his creativity into other forms. He brings a sense of architecture and modernity to his signature textile appliqué language, inspired by Korean pojagi and other historical quilting techniques. He creates compositions with hand-stitched details, pops of unexpected color, unconventional shapes, and unique material combinations. Pogue works together with the design studio Commune on products and special projects using textile remnants and vintage fabrics, including obi fabrics from Japan, upholstery army canvas, and discarded carpet and drapery.

Anthony Akinbola

Brooklyn, New York, and Holmes, New York
b. 1991

"It started with my mom. She studied textile design, and together with my dad they made clothes; they both did batik. My sister also did batik. That was my first exposure to art. I remember the smell of the batik wax and the hot plates in the studio room behind my mom's shop, where she sometimes held workshops. She also painted and did tufting. She was teaching art right up until she passed away."

Anthony Olubunmi Akinbola, born in Columbia, Missouri, is first-generation Nigerian American, raised in both Missouri and Nigeria. Akinbola attended Purchase College in New York and was exposed there to art that was avant-garde and accessible. In 2016 he began his work with durags—cloth scarf caps used with Black hair. Akinbola describes durags as having a political and cultural significance related to Black identity and masculinity. He doesn't sketch prior to sewing; he lays the durags on the floor and sorts them into colors spontaneously. Through his work he unpacks the rituals and histories separating Africa from Black America in an attempt to mitigate that separation. His multifaceted compositions celebrate and reconcile diverse cultural narratives, creating multilayered artworks engaging consumption, respectability, and the commodification of Black culture. Akinbola lives and works in Brooklyn and Upstate New York.

Blair Saxon-Hill

Los Angeles, California
b. 1979

"My mother has a great sense of style with an eye for textiles—she has been an inspirational source in my practice. My great grandmother made quilts, and then the interest in hand-sewing skipped a few generations down to me. I came to work with cloth from a desire to scale up my paper collages that were previously limited to the scale of their source material, the book. Once I resolved to make large-scale fabric collages, the choice of using vintage fabrics was in keeping with my sensibilities. My mother was an antiques dealer, so I grew up with an affinity for used and older things, including textiles, weavings, and basketry."

As a child in Eugene, Oregon, Blair Saxon-Hill saw an appreciation for textiles in her mother, Teryl Saxon-Hill. She studied studio art at Reed College in Portland and received fellowships from the Oregon Arts Commission and the Joan Mitchell Foundation. Now a multidisciplinary artist working in collage, painting, and sculpture, Saxon-Hill's figurative works are queer, pedestrian, and registering current cultural and political realities. She is committed to addressing assumptions around what is considered "normal" within society. As a materials-driven artist, Saxon-Hill most often works with found objects, rare books, and vintage textiles, allowing various materials to inform her construction process. She transmutes the quotidian into a language of her own—buoyant, generative, and idiosyncratic.

OPPOSITE
Grapes, 2022
Fabric collage on canvas-wrapped panel;
77 × 51 inches (196 × 130 cm)

ABOVE
Forks, 2022
Fabric collage on canvas-wrapped panel;
77 × 51 inches (196 × 130 cm)

Cassie McGettigan

Bolinas, California
b. 1982

"My grandmother Jane was an ambitious needlepointer, but I never learned from her. Her guest room was done up in matching blue chintz (on the walls, curtains, and twin bedspreads), and it made an impression on me. My mom brought me along to volunteer at a thrift store. I learned a lot pawing through donation piles, pricing and cherry-picking. That's the first place I encountered a Marimekko shift dress.

"The quilted pieces I've been making lately take on many of the qualities and mechanical riddles I pursued with printed fabric: repetition and deviation, declarative simplicity, overwhelm, decoration, celebration. But instead of presenting a definitive surface, I'm courting more exploration and ambiguity by working dimensionally."

Cassie McGettigan was born in Alexandria, Virginia, and received a BA in Religious Studies from the University of Virginia. After college, she moved to Berkeley, California, and then San Francisco. She was interested in journalism and worked for *7×7* magazine, 826 Valencia, and *Mother Jones*. In 2008, she cofounded Gravel & Gold, a design collective and shop in San Francisco. After years of designing for print, McGettigan wanted to do the screen printing herself. She attended the Rhode Island School of Design for an MFA in Textiles, and she notes that, when she got to RISD, her appetite for all kinds of skills and ideas was voracious. After completing her degree, she stayed for a year to teach fabric silk screen and site-specific installation. She maintains a studio practice, working primarily in fabric silk screening, sewing, and quilting.

Denyse Schmidt

Bridgeport, Connecticut
b. 1961

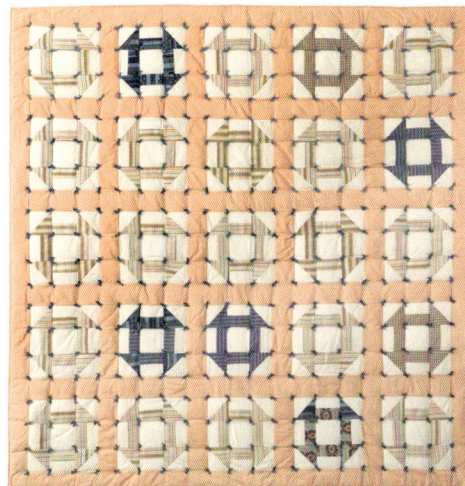

"My mother loved fabric and sewed clothes for herself and four kids (and worked full-time), and my earliest textile-related memories are of fabric shopping with her in the old mill outlets that were prevalent where I grew up. As a kid I sewed toys and clothes and had a few sewing-related jobs over the years. I never expected to end up making quilts for a living, but here I am. I can't imagine doing anything else.

"My mother's grandmother taught her to sew, and I imagine my mother learned to love textiles from her. After I started my business, I learned that this great-grandmother also made quilts. I never knew this, since none of those quilts survived. They had been made from worn-out clothing and were heavily used, and from my mother's description, it sounded like they were utilitarian in design—using fabrics as-is, quickly made to serve a need, and intuitively pieced. I loved learning this; it made me feel I was somehow innately carrying on the work of my ancestors."

Denyse Schmidt was born in an old textile mill town in central Massachusetts. Her parents, having grown up in the Depression, felt that when you needed something, you made it yourself. Schmidt started making things when she was a child and never stopped. She studied graphic design at the Rhode Island School of Design and stumbled across images of improvised, utilitarian quilts in books and journals. Schmidt exhibited her first quilts at a contemporary furniture fair in New York City, with work that channeled her wobbly drawings and quirky color sense. Known as a "modern" quilter, Schmidt actually draws much of her creative vision from quilts of the past and pays homage to the quilters who came before her. Her studio is located in a historic factory building, previously home to the American Fabrics Company, which manufactured lace fabric, trim, and embroideries from 1908 to 1990.

Doris Pettway Mosely

Boykin, Alabama
b. 1959

"My mother made quilts out of old clothes to keep us warm. I started sewing at age fourteen. I made clothes for my sister and brother. Gowns for weddings and proms. I made clothes for my children. I'm a fourth-generation quilter. My daughter quilts when she can. Quilting is a labor of love and a passion."

Born in Gee's Bend, Alabama, Doris Pettway Mosley was taught to sew and quilt at an early age by her mother, Leola Pettway. Although she sometimes helped her mother with her quilting, she did not quilt on her own until she joined the Gee's Bend Quilting Collective at age forty-nine. In 2012, Pettway Mosley started quilting at the Gee's Bend Welcome Center in Boykin, where she enjoys interacting with visitors who ride the ferry across the Alabama River from Camden, Alabama. Pettway Mosley uses both repurposed clothing and new fabric, often choosing bright colors. Her quilt designs are inspired by books, fabrics, and colors.

Elizabeth Brandt

Cincinnati, Ohio
b. 1962

OPPOSITE
Ricochet, 2022
Pieced cotton fabric
and batting, hand-
knotted with cotton
floss; 50½ × 50½
inches (128 × 128 cm)

LEFT
Jump Cut, 2021
Pieced cotton fabric
and batting, hand-
tied with cotton floss;
44 × 37 inches
(112 × 94 cm)

"During frequent visits to Ohio, I discovered the work of Nancy Crow, who lives and teaches nearby. She was the first person I met who used quilt making as an art form, and I was amazed at her bold fabric compositions. I learned improvisational methods from her workshops, and they were the perfect companion to my interest in Buddhist meditation and mindfulness practices. Through Nancy's teaching facility, I also began studying collage with painter David Hornung. Working with him has led me to explore adding more expressive elements into my sewn work. Hand-stitching, knotting, and tying help make the work more individual and add a layer of texture and color, which can be either subtle or bold. The piece can change dramatically until the very end of a project."

As a child in Ohio, Elizabeth Brandt spent hours hand-sewing and embroidering felt animals and ornaments. She rediscovered the practice when her father fell ill, and she would sew while visiting him. In her fifties, she began working full-time as a studio artist, creating improvisational sewn abstractions and paper collages. Brandt remains open by moving different cuts of fabric around to see if something unexpected will happen, and she diligently focuses her attention on the last stages of a project, especially when the repetition and density of stitching can keep her in front of the sewing machine for hours. Through her quilt-making practice, Brandt is reworking a traditional craft that has uniquely represented both artistic expression and utility in tandem.

Faith Ringgold

Englewood, New Jersey
1930–2024

OPPOSITE
Slave Rape #2: Run You Might Get Away, 1972

LEFT
Subway Graffiti #2, 1987

"My great-great-grandmother Susan Shannon and her daughter, my great-grandmother Betsy Bingham, were both born slaves and were quilters all their lives. Both lived into advanced old age in Florida, where they continued, after slavery, to work as quilters and seamstresses. Betsy taught her granddaughter, my mother, Willi Posey, how to quilt, and my mother taught me.

"My first collaboration with my mother was Echoes of Harlem, *made in 1980, one year before she died. I continued to gradually make quilts on my own, producing my first story quilt,* Who's Afraid of Aunt Jemima, *over the course of an entire year as part of my mourning of the loss of my mother. Since then, I always work with collaborators, most recently my assistant Grace Matthews. The idea to make story quilts—that is, painting on canvas framed with quilting and bordered with boxes of text—first came out of my desire to tell my own story and to see my writing in print. Every time I exhibited a story quilt, I was also 'publishing' a story I had written."*

Interview by Osei Bonsu for frieze *magazine in 2018*

Faith Ringgold was raised in Harlem, New York, the youngest of three children and a descendant of the Great Migration—the movement of Black Americans out of the rural South between 1910 and 1970. After the Harlem Renaissance, Ringgold's childhood home was surrounded by a thriving arts scene. She learned to sew from her mother, a fashion designer. Ringgold's great-grandmother, who was enslaved, was a quilter who passed her knowledge to her daughter and granddaughter. In her early forties, Ringgold experienced an influential visit to the Rijksmuseum in Amsterdam, where she saw a collection of fourteenth- and fifteenth-century Nepali paintings that inspired her to develop her narrative quilt paintings with fabric borders. Her artistic practice was widely varied—she was a mixed-media sculptor, performance artist, activist, and author. Her work was greatly affected by the people, poetry, and music she encountered in her childhood, as well as the racism, sexism, and segregation she experienced.

Jonathan Parker

Santa Fe, New Mexico
b. 1952

OPPOSITE
SC #134, 2019
Sewn acrylic on
canvas; 14 × 11 inches
(36 × 28 cm)

ABOVE LEFT
SC #397, 2022
Sewn acrylic
on canvas;
28 × 22 inches
(72 × 56 cm)

ABOVE RIGHT
SC #420, 2023
Sewn acrylic on linen;
14 × 11 inches
(36 × 28 cm)

"I gravitated toward sports as a kid. I only did art in art classes and wasn't particularly good at it. But I enjoyed that it wasn't an academic class, so there wasn't much pressure to excel. When I discovered a passion for art as an adult, my family was encouraging, but not overly so, since they really had no frame of reference for art and artists. The encouragement has always come from within myself."

Jonathan Parker was born in Los Angeles and grew up in the Bay Area. He was not exposed much to art as a kid; his interest began in his late twenties. He credits exposure to art in museums and books as spurring his interest, especially vernacular art like quilts. Many of his friends at the time were working artists who had graduated from the California College of the Arts in Oakland, and they encouraged his work in painting. In the 1990s Parker began sewing gray yoga blankets together to create quilt-like forms. His work caught the attention of gallerist Ruth Braunstein, and his quilts were part of an exhibition at the Braunstein/Quay Gallery in San Francisco. Parker now works by cutting fabrics, sewing pieces together, painting the cloth, then stretching the sewn and painted piece over stretcher bars. His materials incorporate past actions, "fingerprints" of stains, mistakes, and unraveled edges. Parker's work explores shapes, texture, and color—and the interaction between them.

Kathryn Clark

Sonoma, California
b. 1971

"My interest in textiles has its roots in my parents' background, my mother being an artist and my father an architect; they crossed paths in Alabama in the late 1950s and bonded over a love of Bauhaus design. I grew up surrounded by handmade treasures: my mom's woven textiles and stained glass, my dad's pottery and hand-carved wood objects. We had a five-foot-wide floor loom set up in our family room. My mother died when I was a teenager, so we never had direct conversations about art, but my memories of her weaving are strong, and I think this is where my comfort with textiles originates."

Originally from Knoxville, Tennessee, Kathryn Clark spent her formative years in North Florida, Georgia, and Alabama before moving to San Francisco in her twenties. Spanning these diverse regions made her sensitive to cultural differences and divisions. A passion for the social benefits of urban planning and a fascination with maps led her to work for Peter Calthorpe, a visionary in the field of urban planning. Early in her career, Clark shifted her passion for sociology and geography into her art practice. She draws from her background as an urban planner and architect, using factual data to reveal our environment and architectural pillars of society as fragile existences that are being picked apart and torn down. She is intrigued by the architectural possibilities of fabric using only needle and thread.

Kiva Motnyk

Manhattan, New York, and Woodstock, New York
b. 1977

"I was trained in many different ways: through growing up with a creative, artistic family, studying at art school, and working in the design world for many years. At some point I needed to unlearn the rules I had been taught and learn to listen to my instincts. When I opened the studio, that was the hardest thing for me to do: unlearn all the ways I thought I was supposed to do things. But I do think it's important to learn the traditional techniques, initially, so that you have the tools to expand your own work."

Kiva Motnyk spent her childhood shifting between her family home in San Francisco, California, and a converted loft in SoHo in Manhattan. Her father was a painter, her mother a dancer. There was little separation in the family's work and life, and early on Motnyk was exposed to shared creative energy. She studied fashion and textile design at the Rhode Island School of Design and then, after returning to New York, worked in the fashion industry. In 2014, she started Thompson Street Studio. Motnyk's work in textiles reinterprets historical and cultural traditions of making, through modernist abstraction. Her sensibility is rooted in a love of color, texture, and pattern expressed in a modern application of traditional techniques: silk-screening, weaving, knitting, quilting, and multiple dye methods. Motnyk aims to preserve and bring recognition to textile heritage. She focuses on using recycled materials and antique fabrics, creating a dialogue between historic and new. She likes to spend time in the country, where she finds inspiration from nature's materials and colors.

OPPOSITE AND ABOVE
Talismans, 2023
Pieced patchwork with appliqué, embroidery, and hand quilting using mixed remnant fabric; 68 × 49 inches (173 × 125 cm)

Kristen Lombardi

Boston, Massachusetts
b. 1979

Two years ago, I took the train from New York to Boston and met Kristen at the Massachusetts College of Art and Design, where she teaches. At the school's art museum, we had a private tour of *Designing Motherhood: Things That Make and Break Our Births*, curated by my friend Michelle Millar Fisher. Kristen and I caught up on life, work, and parenthood as we walked through the groundbreaking exhibit. Upstairs we viewed the impressively large work of Portuguese textile artist Joana Vasconcelos.

—Lena

OPPOSITE AND ABOVE
Sewn leather remnants;
12 × 12 inches
(30 × 30 cm)

"Textile work is inside me. I grew up with a mom who is an expert sewer and a dad who can take things apart and fix them—two creative and practical problem-solvers. Creating textiles (as I have done over many years) happened slowly, organically, and out of the desire to use scraps. It has now become my focus, and I'm so happy working this way. I love process. I have begun to see myself more and more as a link in a chain of people who make things, undo things, mend things, and consider how things are made."

Rhode Island native Kristen Lombardi began sewing at a young age, using patterns in her mother's workroom and making wreaths from scrap fabric. She is a graduate of the Massachusetts College of Art and Design's Fashion Design program, where she also teaches. Lombardi specializes in working with leather as a material, and she prioritizes saving scrap leather from waste. The jump from using woven material to animal hide came after a trip to the Southwest with a friend, where they saw traditional Native American handcrafts and leather goods. Lombardi formed Manimal, a soft-leather boot company, in 2003. Her work is an exploration of color, form, and process. Taking cues from nature and handcrafting traditions, Lombardi designs pieces to be well-worn and long-lasting. She considers her use of leather (a precious material) to come with responsibility, and she is dedicated to no waste. She sources her leather from secondhand shops and a wholesale company in California where all hides are meat-industry byproduct.

Magnus Maxine

Pasadena, California
b. 1985

OPPOSITE
Quilt I, 2018–2021
Cotton, linen, and
nylon with avocado,
turmeric, weld, and
indigo; 81 × 63 inches
(206 × 160 cm)

LEFT
Quilt II, 2018–2021
Cotton, linen, and
nylon with avocado,
logwood, weld, indigo,
and found material;
81 × 63 inches
(206 × 160 cm)

"My great-great-grandmother on my mother's side is from the Blackfeet Nation. Her name was Muse, and she traveled to the Southwest after meeting my great-great-grandfather. She settled there and made a family.

"I have always been drawn to quilts and quilting for the storytelling and refined labor and skills of the makers. I remember seeing Rosie Lee Tompkins's quilts and resonating with her relationship to the medium. They are so powerful and poetic. Another aspect of quilting I find compelling is that many of the most famous and beloved makers are unknown. The materials tell us stories."

Magnus Maxine was born in Juneau, Alaska, and lived in a small neighborhood adjacent to Mendenhall Glacier. She has fond memories of climbing trees, ice fishing, and picking wild blueberries in Alaska. In sixth grade, having moved to Utah, she learned how to sew in home economics class, and she began altering her clothes. Maxine received a BFA from the California Institute of the Arts in Santa Clarita, California, in 2013. She now works in her outdoor studio to process natural, plant-based dyes, with results fluctuating due to weather and environmental changes. Her quilts are cut and sewn with bedding from military barracks and the Los Angeles prison system. By reworking these materials, combined with traditional natural-dyeing methods, she creates new information and meaning—and pays homage to the invisible labor of oppressed peoples. In her paintings and quilts, Maxine explores dichotomies of shapes and textures. She has published several books, including *Arise in Your Might and Protest This Damnable Outrage* in 2017.

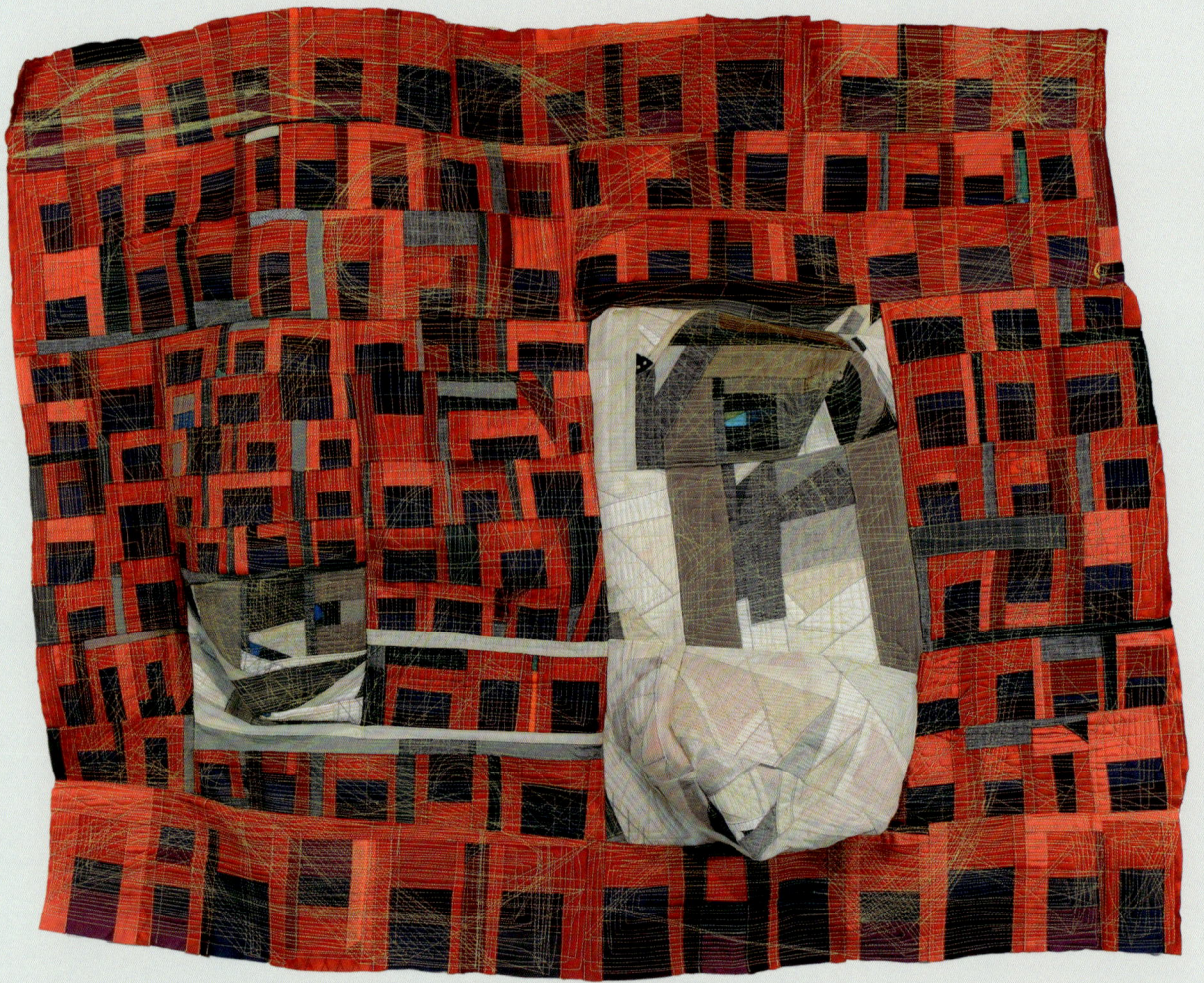

Mansur Nurullah

San Francisco, California
b. 1973

OPPOSITE
Love, Luck, and Supports, 2017
Scavenged material: Cordura, upholstery fabric, nylon thread, batting, and grommets; 39 × 52 inches (99 × 132 cm)

ABOVE
Imagined Migration Route of My Maternal Great-Grandparents to Chicago, 2019
Scavenged material: awning fabric, IKEA bags, firefighter uniforms, welding curtain, and upholstery fabric; 86 × 108 inches (218 × 274 cm)

"As I sew, patterns and shapes slowly emerge, providing a sense of direction for viewers and myself. The process is intuitive, with little or no planning involved. An important element of my practice is the source material. The materials that I use most often are discarded textiles, gleaned from local outdoor equipment producers. My art may also contain leather from abandoned couches, fallen road signs, upholstery samples, and disassembled elements of shoes and purses carefully placed by the curb for disposal. I collect rosemary, sage, eucalyptus, Mexican marigold, chamomile, and other aromatic plants to use between layers of fabric."

Born in Chicago, Illinois, Mansur Nurullah grew up understanding the city through public transportation and walking. In his work, Nurullah examines his maternal great-grandparents' migration to Chicago after episodes of racial violence in the Jim Crow South drove them north. Nurullah depicted their trek in a 6 × 9-foot (15 × 23 cm) quilt, composed of materials including welding curtains, awnings, upholstery, leather, and uniforms. His pieces are informed by the natural environment, architecture, memory, history, imagination, and process. Nurullah transforms materials that are bound for the trash. He makes intricate, large-scale textile works that reference travel and navigation, often representing his own journeys—both literal (transportation by bike) and metaphorical (as an artist and counselor who came to his career through nontraditional paths).

Maura Ambrose

Bastrop, Texas
b. 1982

OPPOSITE
Railroad Denim Quilt
Made with vintage
railroad denim
overalls, hand-quilted
with Japanese
sashiko thread;
63 × 51 inches
(160 × 130 cm)

ABOVE
Pine Cone Star
Indigo-dyed linen and
cotton, hand-quilted
and hand-stitched
binding; 97 × 97
inches (146 × 146 cm)

"My great-aunts made quilts, and all the women on my mother's side of the family made their own clothes. My relationship to textiles and cloth is a calling and passion that manifested into a career."

Raised in Middletown, Maryland, Maura Ambrose was encouraged to work with cloth by her grandmother and mother, both of whom made their own clothes and home-wares. Later, she found the professors in the Fibers Department at Savannah College of Art and Design to be her greatest teachers of the history and hands-on processes of making textiles. Ambrose founded Folk Fibers in her twenties, during a creatively charged summer road trip, and she followed her dream to combine gardening and quilting. It brings Ambrose joy and meaning to connect with ancestors through the work, and carry on the tradition of heritage crafts. She has shared her process of yielding dye from plants and using those colors for quilt making. Her studio and garden, on ten woodland acres by the lower Colorado River, are a sanctuary of color where the work begins and develops a sympathetic approach to color, from seed, to plant, to dye, to textile.

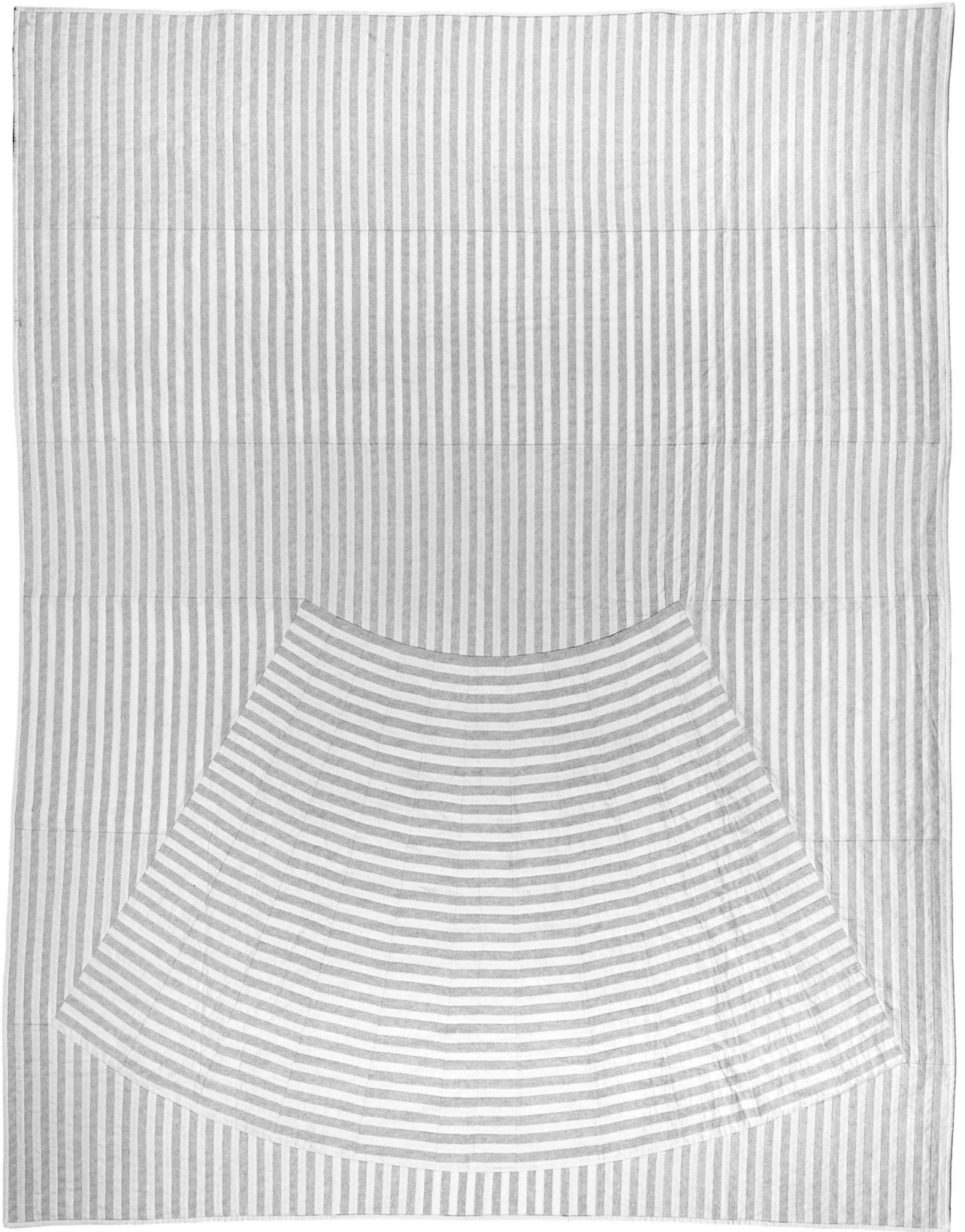

Meg Callahan

Providence, Rhode Island
b. 1988

OPPOSITE
Mahler Quilt
Cotton fabric and
cotton batting

ABOVE
Maui Quilt
Cotton fabric and
cotton batting

"My mom, Margie Callahan, is an architect and painter, and because of her, I was exposed and had access to tools (circle templates, scale rulers, light tables, jars of pencils) and to creative environments. When I became interested in sewing, she pulled out an old sewing machine she had received as a wedding gift (and never used). My family was very supportive of creative pursuits and gave us freedom to explore, try, fail, try again.

"I learned from wonderful female quilters and had a (sort of) late-in-life discovery of the history and traditions of quilting. It is a fascinating craft and has roots in community/communal making in which sharing ideas, techniques, and patterns are commonplace. In that way, though it was not something I shared with my family, I feel part of a lineage of makers."

Raised in Oklahoma, Meg Callahan had access to quilting tools (a sewing machine, circle templates, and scale rulers) at a young age from her mother. Now, alongside her studio practice, she teaches furniture design at the Rhode Island School of Design and runs M.Callahan Studio. Her studio is dedicated to creating objects that focus on the beauty and complexity of construction, mainly through patchwork quilting. Her work is a culmination of traditional processes and experimentation, and it looks to the contemporary potential of craft traditions. In her teaching work, Callahan uses primarily wood as a material, but feels she is always engaging in connections between material, craft, design, object, and human interaction.

OCCIDENTAL COLLEGE–COLUMBIA UNIVERSITY
LAW DEGREE HARVARD–UNITED STATES SENATOR
COMMUNITY ORGANIZING HOUSING PROJECTS 1985
"WE HOLD THESE TRUTHS TO BE SELF EVIDENT, JULY 4
THAT ALL MEN ARE CREATED EQUAL" 1776

DREAMS OF MY FATHER 1972

THE AUDACITY OF HOPE 1992

ATLANTIC OCEAN

PACIFIC OCEAN

KENYA

KANSAS

44

16

BARACK HUSSEIN OBAMA 2nd AUGUST 4 1961
ANN DUNHAM–MOTHER– HONOLULU, HAWAII
LIVED JAKARTA INDONESIA–LOS ANGELES
NEW YORK– BOSTON–CHICAGO–WASHINGTON D.C.

MICHAEL A. CUMMINGS 5-30-09

Michael A. Cummings

Harlem, New York
b. 1945

OPPOSITE
A Young Obama,
2009
Machine sewn,
cotton fabrics

ABOVE
Waiting for Slave Ship
Henrietta Marie
Machine sewn,
cotton fabrics

"Over the years as I developed my art skills, I began to realize how politicized art was and how it was used to elevate some people and exclude others. I just wanted to be an artist; however, living in America as a person of color, I had to be labeled an African American artist, not just an artist. American (white) art historians and critics could easily continue to omit all African American artists from their version of art history. I am proud to be African American, and now my new given description/name is Black artist. Racism has prevented the public from knowing about great Black artists.

"I accidentally discovered how textiles could provide instant colors and prints without having to mix paints. I knew nothing about textiles and sewing machines. While making my first textile composition, I fell in love with the process. The first half of developing a quilt is magical, because I am transferring my visual idea into a tangible item. The second half of the process is exciting because I see the quilt coming together—and reaching completion is amazing."

Michael A. Cummings grew up in Los Angeles, California, and earned a BA in American Art History at Empire College. He moved to New York in the early 1970s to take a position with the New York City Department of Cultural Affairs. Cummings spent his early artistic career as a part-time collage and paint artist. After a work project to create a cloth banner for an exhibition in 1973, Cummings discovered his love for working with fabric and taught himself to quilt by studying the works of local quilters and how-to quilt magazines and books. His work features bright, colorful fabric, and historical themes that honor a narrative, storytelling tradition. Cummings is a founding member of the Women of Color Quilters Network, founded by Carolyn L. Mazloomi.

Niki Tsukamoto

Los Angeles, California
b. 1974

OPPOSITE
AND ABOVE
Two flags paired as a
single work, titled
*Absolute Magnitude:
Knowing, Ignorance,
and Being,* 2016
Naturally dyed and
appliquéd flags

"My maternal foremothers all worked with cloth. My great-grandmother and grandmother taught me from a very young age how to cut and sew, [along with] pattern making, crochet, embroidery, all of it. They were working-class people and learned all of these skills through necessity. If they wanted nice things, they needed to make them themselves. I've now come to realize as an adult that they were wildly talented. Some of my most treasured memories are afternoons spent crocheting squares or learning embroidery stitches with them."

Born in Indiana, Niki Tsukamoto was taught to sew at age four by her great-grandmother, who also introduced her to dye plants. Tsukamoto began experimenting with natural medicine from an early age because of her chronic health issues. She studied medicine in college but left to pursue herbalism and bodywork. She met her partner and creative collaborator, Yusuke, when she visited his artist studio, having been introduced by a mutual friend. Together they work under the name Lookout & Wonderland Workshop, an inspiration center for their personal art practice, artistic collaboration, contemplation, and making of handcrafted goods. They are deeply informed by the essence of the avant-garde art movements Vienna Secession, Wiener Werkstätte, and Gesamtkunstwerk. Niki considers their work a devotional practice and a meditative ritual.

Pat Gorelangton

Waikiki, Hawaii
b. 1952

"My Filipino grandmother did fine crochet work, and it was mesmerizing to watch. I think my love of hand stitching came from her. My mother taught me to sew when I was a teenager, so I was comfortable with a sewing machine and was hand-sewing hems at a relatively young age. When I joined the Poakalani quilt group seventeen years ago, Hawaiian quilting became my passion. I made Hawaiian quilts before that, and even designed patterns, but I would say that joining that group, and being exposed to the artistry of John Serrao and the loving ohana spirit of his family, has fed my quilting soul immeasurably. I can't imagine doing anything else. John is sorely missed."

As a mother to young kids, Hawaiian native Pat Gorelangton sought out quilting as a quiet time for herself. She studied with master quilt-pattern designer John Serrao, who encouraged her to create her own patterns, in addition to quilting his designs. Since she began, Gorelangton estimates that she has made close to 150 quilts. She works with cotton fabric and sometimes incorporates batik-dyed fabric. Gorelangton notes how quilting makes cloth three-dimensional; it is a tactile art that can be appreciated visually, but also by touch. Her green and yellow *Hula Girl Hibiscus* quilt (opposite) is a contemporary Hawaiian quilt design, since the yellow fabric is behind the green fabric, using reverse appliqué. Traditional Hawaiian quilting has the pattern fabric on top of the background fabric. Upon finishing a quilt, Gorelangton spends a night sleeping under it so that her spiritual energy, mana, can pass on to the new owner.

Pauline Boyd

Los Angeles, California
b. 1979

"My ancestry is Scottish and Irish—so a deep connection there to fiber and craft. My mother was the type to hang bits of textiles everywhere. Aesthetically I grew up with gorgeous things thumbtacked on the wall. My father was very connected to cloth in the way that it bonded him to his mother and grandmother. I think I internalized from him a sense of validation that working with cloth was kind of a spiritual experience and an act of service and care, necessary for your family and community.

"Making a quilt is such a long process. I go through a whole host of feelings with it—sometimes obsessed, sometimes hating it, sometimes staring and touching every little piece in adoration, and then ultimately wondering how I got it done. I try to start each piece from a place of necessity and utility, and I set little 'rules' for the composition, which I inevitably come up against and have to find solutions for in order to stay on track. In this way, I keep it active for myself; it's a labor of love, a constant renewing and revisiting of purpose."

As a child in Los Angeles, Pauline Boyd was interested in theater arts and film. Later, as a teen, she loved making collages and experimented with hand-sewing projects. On a trip to visit family friends in Arkansas in 2004, Boyd was struck by their passion for quilting. After returning home, she bought a sewing machine (she had never used one) and made her first quilt. Then living in New York City and with no fabric yardage to use, she cut up sheets, curtains, and clothes. Later, travel to Cambodia and Laos deeply influenced her work. She established her soft-furnishings studio, Counterpane, in Los Angeles around 2012 and continues to make quilts—all one-of-a-kind pieces with bits of things she finds traveling: old clothes, vintage, deadstock material, or excess garment fabric.

OPPOSITE
Dresden Variation II, 2021
Cotton remnants; 60 × 60 inches
(152 × 152 cm)

ABOVE
Dresden Variation III, 2023
Cotton and silk remnants; 60 × 60 inches
(152 × 152 cm)

Rachel Meade Smith

Brooklyn, New York
b. 1988

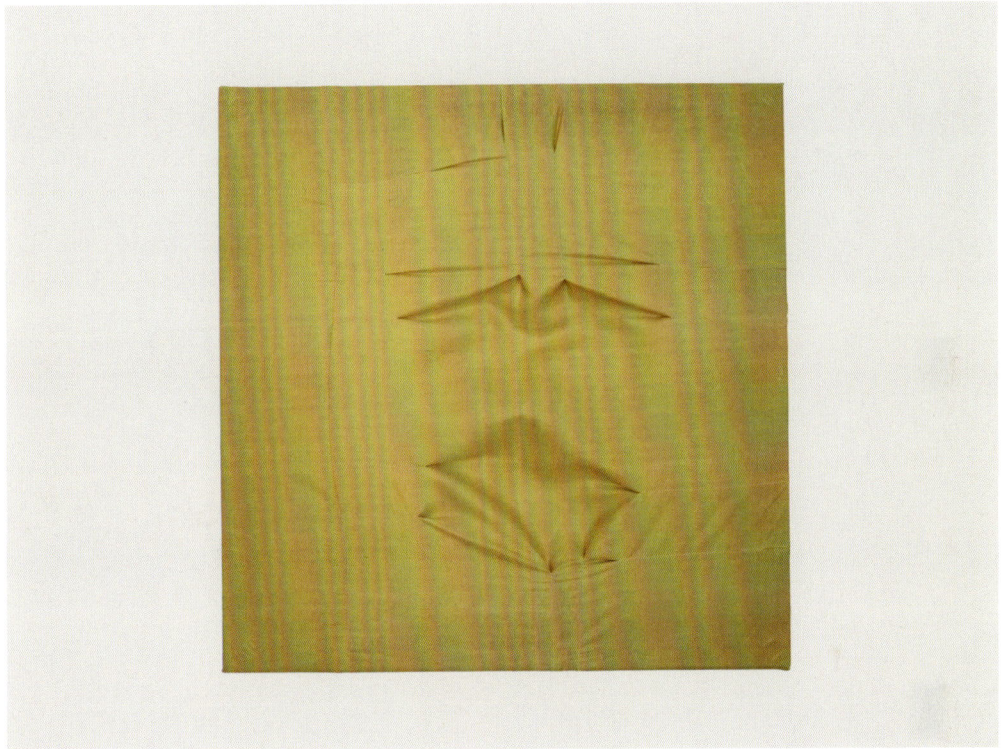

OPPOSITE
Red Terrain, 2023
Cotton and found
frame; 20 × 16 inches
(51 × 41 cm)

ABOVE
Yellow Terrain, 2023
Silk, cotton thread,
and found frame;
18 × 18 inches
(46 × 46 cm)

"Over the last decade or so I've moved between different techniques, from leatherworking to tufting, weaving, basketry, net making, mending, knitting, sewing, and quilting, roughly in that order, and playing with so many kinds of materials—wool, cotton, sisal, rope, fabric scraps, parchment paper, photographs. I get an idea for a shape or a texture and move impulsively toward it; sometimes that means learning something new or returning to a technique I haven't touched in a long time. My practice has grown in fits and starts, and mostly thanks to my own obsessive tendencies."

Rachel Meade Smith started altering her own clothes as a kid because of her small size; nothing fit. As a teenager she spent weekends going to flea markets and taking classes at the Fashion Institute of Technology in New York City, where she learned the basics of using a sewing machine. Her college essay was written about her love for secondhand clothes. She now works as an editor, researcher, and artist. Her textile art practice involves using mostly damaged, discarded, and found materials, and her creative practice spans textiles, paper-based media, and oral history. She has developed and taught mending workshops around the world. Her relationship with cloth and textiles was based on impulse and instinct, and also necessity.

Sarah Nsikak

Brooklyn, New York
b. 1991

"*Africa is where so many brilliant modalities of fiber art began, spanning the spectrum of form and function, and I wanted to create a project that would pay tribute to that. My many muses, from my Nigerian seamstress grandmother to the artists of Gee's Bend, have made so much beauty out of waste. Honoring the planet, while preserving traditional ways of doing and making, is the axis of purpose and meaning for me. I have always felt that art was at the center of my work, no matter what form it takes—and maybe I'll always oscillate between designing wearable art and making large-scale art pieces as the center of my work. I feel the most in touch with who I am as an individual and my creative voice when I'm making tapestry art pieces.*"

Sarah Nsikak is Nigerian American, born in Oklahoma. She learned to sew at a young age by reproducing patterns from mail-order catalogs. Her love of textiles led her to work in the fashion industry for several years after completing a master's degree in Art Therapy. Observing the waste generated in the fashion industry inspired a pivot to her art practice. Nsikak's hand-quilted pieces are made exclusively using recycled material sourced from fashion designers based in New York. The name of her brand, La Réunion—initially named after the island east of Madagascar—carries many meanings. Her influences for this project include the vibrant stories of African culture, postcolonial African exuberance, and ideas surrounding reclaimed beauty, togetherness, and joy.

Season Evans

Seattle, Washington
b. 1979

"I spent time with my grandparents, who lived in another state, during the summers when I was a kid. My grandmother taught me to use a sewing machine when I was about eight. We would go to a fabric store and pick out a pattern to make a piece of clothing together. But I didn't have a sewing machine at home, and so I only sewed when I was with her. She was the first person to validate my joy in making."

As a child in southeastern Pennsylvania, Season Evans loved to draw and make crafts. She identifies as a lifelong maker. During undergraduate studies in rural Pennsylvania, she discovered quilts as something greater than objects: pieces of art with stories told in cloth. Evans creates functional quilts, patchwork art pieces, and site-specific installations. Rooted in traditional quilt making and with a dedication to craft, she sees quilts as objects and as storytellers, using the simplicity of line and the essentials of geometry to create visual depictions of everyday life. For Evans, the quilt-making process becomes a meditation (intimate, tactile, and repetitive). She sees the goal of her work as focusing on narrative, using the essential elements of a pattern and material. Evans teaches various quilting workshops.

Sharon Pettway Williams

Boykin, Alabama
b. 1958

"I used to sit and watch my mother sew. She would be sewing and cooking at the same time. Every once in a while, she would go to check on her food, and I would get up on the quilt and start making stitches."

Sharon Pettway Williams was born into the tight-knit Gee's Bend community, surrounded on three sides by the Alabama River and inhabited mostly by descendants of enslaved Africans on the Pettway Plantation. The tradition of quilt making that developed in Gee's Bend traces back to the earliest days of the plantation, drawing from a combination of African, Native American, and original techniques. The quilts first came to national attention in the 1960s with the formation of the Freedom Quilting Bee. The collective was a way for women in the community to earn money and rally support for the voting drives of the Civil Rights Movement. Pettway Williams has been sewing for as long as she can remember. She quilts every day with her daughter and granddaughter.

Zak Foster

Clemmons, North Carolina, and Brooklyn, New York
b. 1980

"My work over the last few years has centered on memory quilts and, more recently, burial quilts. I remember hearing a story on the radio, years ago, about a woman who passed away, and (in accordance to her last wishes) her friends wrapped her body up in her favorite quilt, drove out to the middle of the woods, and buried her. I remember thinking at the time: That's how I want to go. And I'm sure I'm not alone in that.

"My vision is to create quilts that are cherished in life, and then when the day comes, this same well-loved quilt can be used in lieu of a casket (just roll the body in a soft and colorful quilt, and return it to the earth). I have my own burial quilt already designed, and just seeing it sitting folded up in the corner of my bedroom every day not only gives me a peace of mind knowing that it's ready, but it also grounds me in the awareness that our days are so fleeting, so each day is an opportunity to create the world we all want to live in while we can."

Zak Foster's earliest textile memory, from his childhood in North Carolina, is watching his grandmother sew clothing. Foster was a public-school teacher for nearly two decades, the last ten years of which he was teaching during the day and establishing himself in the quilt world on the weekends and during school vacations. He is now a full-time artist and community organizer. Foster loves working with repurposed materials so that nothing is wasted. His biggest quilting influences have been the women working in what is now called improvisational quilting—including Irene Williams and Loretta Pettway Bennett. His community the Quilty Nook connects and inspires quilters all over the world.

Suncatcher Patchwork

This project is inspired by *pojagi* (also referred to as *bojagi*), the ancient Korean folk tradition of sewing textiles for both everyday and ceremonial use. *Jogakbo* (or *chogakpo*) means "small segments" in Korean and is the style of patchwork used to create pojagi from scraps of leftover fabrics. I'm very drawn to the graphic seam lines of Pojagi patchwork. The patchwork is reversible, and the seams are totally finished on both sides. There is no backing, and the technique encloses all raw edges. I hang these panels in front of a window, similar to stained glass.

MATERIALS

Lightweight scrap fabric pieces
Straight pins
Sewing machine or needle and thread
Iron and ironing surface
Scissors or a rotary cutter

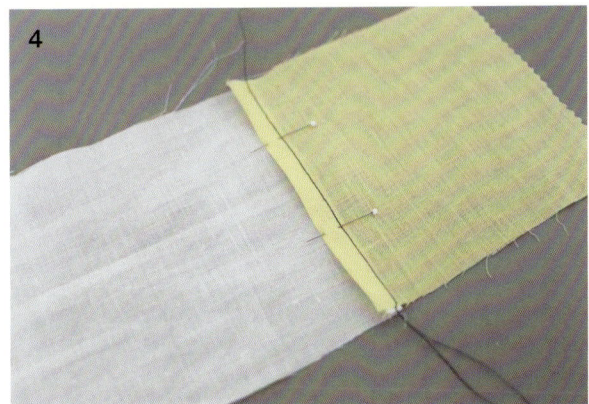

NOTE: *Use scraps of lightweight fabric (left over from other projects or discarded clothing) to experiment with creating a patchwork piece approximately 16 × 20 inches (40.5 × 51 cm). I used contrasting fabric and thread in the instructional photographs for better visibility.*

INSTRUCTIONS

1. Choose two pieces of scrap fabric similar in size. Lay the fabric pieces together with the edges offset by about ½ inch (12 mm).

2. Sew a straight stitch ⅛ inch (3mm) from the raw edge of the folded (yellow) fabric.

3. Fold the raw edge of the bottom (yellow) piece over the edge of the top (white) piece. Press with an iron, and place straight pins.

4. Open the sewn fabric pieces and lay them flat. Press the folded seam allowance over to cover the raw edge. Press with the iron, and add straight pins.

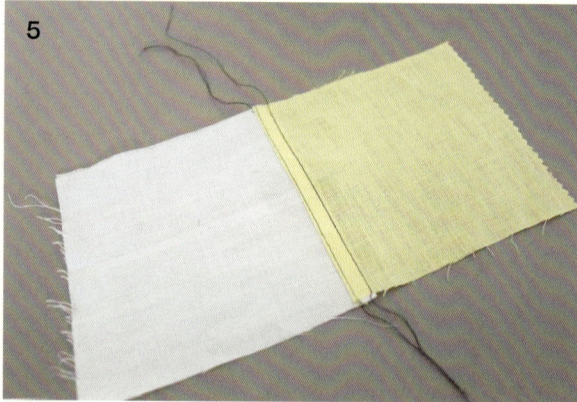

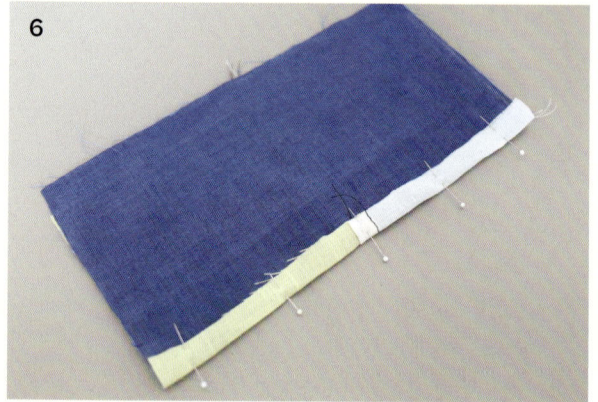

5.   Topstitch the pressed edge ⅛ inch (3mm) from the fold, enclosing all the raw edges.

6.   Choose another piece of scrap fabric (trim as needed) and repeat steps 1 and 2 to add the new piece to the sewn patchwork.

7.   Again, topstitch the pressed edge ⅛ inch (3mm) from the fold, to enclose the raw edges.

8.   Continue growing the patchwork by adding fabric outward. Optional: add a folded end piece, sewn to allow a dowel for hanging.

Relaxed Quilt Squares

A quilting class with artist Denyse Schmidt (page 83) taught me a great lesson on loosening up in my design work. She instructed students to quickly pull strips of scrap fabric from a large pile in the center of the work table, without choosing, and sew them together. Rather than laboring over our color and pattern combinations, we were told to dive in without worry (so uncomfortable!). When we hung the finished squares on the wall, they all looked great individually and especially together. I carried this exercise into my work as a textile designer and photographer.

MATERIALS

Quilting-weight scrap fabric cut into strips approximately 1–5 inches (2.5–13 cm) wide

Basket or paper bag

Straight pins

Sewing machine

Iron and ironing surface

NOTE: *Sew four quilt squares, approximately 10 × 10 inches (25 × 25 cm), using Denyse's improvisational piecing technique of pulling pieces without looking. Use a mix of colors and patterns (can be subtle or bold mixes). The goal is not to create a finished piece, but to play with letting go of expectations and rigidity in a sewing project.*

INSTRUCTIONS

1. Place fabric scraps in a basket or paper bag. Without looking, pull two fabric pieces.

2. Line up the fabric edges, with the right sides together. Trim fabric as needed. Use straight pins to hold the pieces in place.

3. Sew a straight seam with a ¼-inch (6 mm) seam allowance.

4. Open the sewn pieces and press the seams open with the iron, on the wrong side.

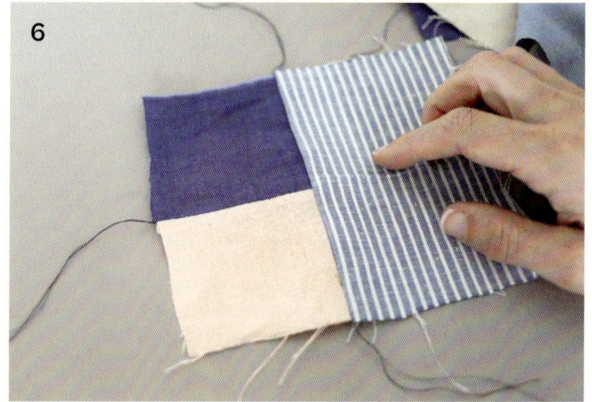

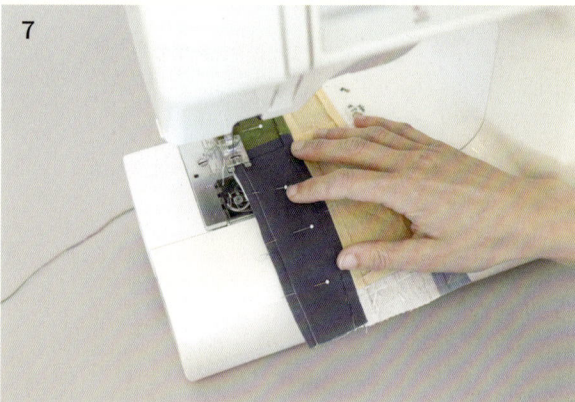

5. Pull a third piece of fabric from the bag and pin it to the wrong side of the first two sewn pieces.

6. Sew a straight seam with a ¼-inch (6 mm) seam allowance to attach the new piece to the growing patchwork. On the wrong side, press the seams open with the iron.

7. Continue pulling pieces and sewing them to the growing patchwork, from the inside outward

8. Continue opening the seams and pressing them with the iron on the wrong side.

Loop and Felt

Intertwine

KNOTTING, KNITTING, and CROCHETING are methods of looping fibers to create cloth. Knotting is done by hand, without a tool, by looping fiber to change its shape. The primary knots are the square or "reef" knot, and forms of the hitch knot (looping several working cords onto a single cord). Knitting uses two or more needles to interlace loops of spun fiber. There are only two basic knit stitches: knit and purl. But there are many thousands of different identified stitch patterns (arrangements of knit and purl stitches), including rib stitch, garter stitch, moss stitch, Stockinette stitch, seed stitch, and waffle stitch. Knitting can be worked flat or "in the round," where one or two circular needles or four or five double-pointed needles are used to create a continuous seamless tube. Crocheting uses a single hook ("crochet" is the French word for hook) to interlock loops of spun fiber, resulting in a piece that is generally thicker and stiffer compared with knitted cloth. The building-block stitches for crochet are chain stitch, single stitch, double stitch, half double stitch, treble stitch, and slip stitch. Free-form crochet is a technique of creating three-dimensional shapes, and this is made possible because new stitches can begin independently of previous stitches, anywhere on the piece. Structural elements can be formed in a way that is not easily done with knitted cloth.

HOOKING and TUFTING are methods of looping fibers through a woven base material like burlap or linen to create a textured cloth. Punch needle hooking (also called rug hooking) creates a knobby texture with lengths of yarn or fabric, and latch hooking creates a shaggy texture using cut pieces of material. Both use a basic tool with a wood handle and metal hook. Tufting requires a tufting tool, typically a tufting gun; a handheld machine in which yarn is fed through a needle and subsequently punched in rapid succession through the base fabric. Electric tufting guns can be cut-pile, loop-pile, or a combination of both.

FELTING is the world's oldest cloth-making technique. It's likely that felting was first discovered by observation. Possibly in an abandoned rabbit's den, someone noticed a small, matted piece of cloth created by the natural combination of fibers, moisture, and agitation. Felt is made in two ways: wet felting and needle felting. Wet felting occurs when moisture and warmth are applied to animal fibers, followed by agitation. These steps create a process that opens the shaft of the fiber, allowing it to become permanently interlocked and fused with other fibers, resulting in a dense cloth. Needle felting uses a long, thin needle that has a series of notches at its tip.

When the needle is poked into the animal fibers repeatedly, the needle notches tangle the fibers together. Animal fibers typically used for felting include wool (sheep), angora (rabbit), mohair (goat), and the fleece from alpacas and llamas. Fibers are classified by micron count, which measures the diameter (from fine to coarse) of a single fiber. The type of fiber and the micron count determine the finished felt's feel and appearance. Raw fiber is sheared from the animal and has not been washed or combed. This is called "in the grease" because of the natural lanolin oils on the fiber from the animal. Washed fiber has been washed of lanolin but can still be uncombed, maintaining the locks from the animal. Top and roving fibers are the most common kinds of fiber found at a store. These fibers have been washed and processed so that they form a clean rope of fibers that are ready to be felted.

Knotting, Knitting, and Crochet Traditions

Indigenous people worldwide used methods of looping fibers to create practical goods like sacks and nets, and decorative items like headgear and ceremonial garments. The Victoria and Albert Museum in England has in its collection a pair of Egyptian socks dating from 250 to 420 CE, made with the early knitting technique *nålbindning*, a Danish term that translates to "needle-binding" and was likely the forerunner to knitting. Historians track the development of knitting to Egypt and Syria from 500 to 1200 CE. Knitting was then spread to Europe by Mediterranean trade routes in the 1300s, and later to the Americas in the 1700 and 1800s. Knitting with wool has been an important part of cultural clothing in the colder climates of the world. On the Scottish Isles during the 1600s, entire families were involved in making sweaters and socks. Elaborate colorful patterns were created on the remote island of Fair Isle in northern Scotland. Knitting by native Salish in the Cowichan Valley of Canada (southeastern Vancouver Island) began shortly after contact with Europeans. They developed their own distinct Cowichan patterns (some learned from Fair Isle knitters), made with thick, handspun, one-ply, natural-colored yarn.

In 1589, English inventor William Lee created the knitting machine, a large frame similar to a weaver's frame that used barbed needles to hold the stitches. In 1759, a patent was given to Jedediah Strutt, who developed the ribber attachment, allowing for more stitch options. Today, knitting machines still use the original basic design. Similar to knitting, the exact origin of crochet is unknown. In 1822, the Dutch needle arts magazine *Penélopé* was the first to refer to crochet as a craft. In 1845, as Ireland entered their Great Famine, some families were able to avoid starvation by starting businesses of crocheting lace. The first patent for a crochet needle was in 1847. The tapestry crochet technique evolved in northern Europe, where Scandinavian crocheters might have been the first to develop the single crochet stitch, allowing a second color to be carried within the stitch.

Hooking and Tufting Traditions

Textile historians believe that people of ancient Egypt and China used methods of looping fibers through a fabric backing. Research also indicates that Vikings in Scandinavia used a technique of hooking wool loops through a base fabric. The more recent history of hooked rugs began in England during the early 1800s. Workers in weaving mills were allowed to collect scrap pieces of yarn. Weavers took them home and pulled the scraps through a backing to create a thicker usable cloth. Colonial settlers to New England brought rug hooking skills from Europe. In the early to mid-1800s, sheep farms were common in New Hampshire, and spun wool provided scraps for hooking. From the mid-1800s to early 1900s, textile mills sold "end cuts" of woven fabric, and poorer families used textile scraps to make their own hooked projects. After the Civil War, rug hooking reached a wider audience when new printed techniques allowed for rug patterns to be printed onto burlap. Later, during the 1930s, latch hooked wool rugs became popular, and written guidelines helped standardize the craft.

Felting Traditions

The earliest evidence of felt dates back to 6500 BCE in the Middle East and Asia, where felting was important to the nomadic tribes for shelter and clothing. In Siberia and Mongolia, felt-making spread across land through the Turkic-Mongolian tribes, who used fibers from sheep and camel. Felt was and is used worldwide, but especially in colder climates like in Scandinavia and Slovenia, where thick cloth is needed. Before people began weaving and sewing, felt was a valued material for being naturally fire-retardant, water-repellent, and sound-dampening, as well as being a natural insulator. Kristina Foley (page 165) talked about why she is drawn to felting wool—"Choosing wool as my medium is a way to deepen my relationship to a specific place and its fibershed. I connect with local farms and their relative challenges and supply chains, as well as seek to understand why a fiber is valued or, if not, how it can be diversely utilized. I ultimately enjoy creating with a material that is innately beautiful, functional, and enduring. Felted wool is simultaneously ancient and unexplored." And Sagarika Sundaram (page 177) talks about her art practice: "My material, my way of felting, traces a lineage of makers spanning fifteen thousand years. Through my work, I'm looking for our shared fingerprint."

OPPOSITE
felted wool by Kristina Foley (page 165)

Akiko Kotani

Gulfport, Florida
b. 1940

OPPOSITE
Waterfalls, 2019
Crocheted
polyethylene;
20 × 20 × 13 feet
(6 × 6 × 4 meters)

ABOVE
Berber series, 1981
Wool over linen
tapestry; 141 × 45–
inch (358 × 114 cm)
panels

"My mother always had yarn on her lap, fashioning items with her hands. Because of this distinct memory, it is natural that as a developing artist the use of soft materials (with manipulation of my hands) became a reality. Two prominent persons in the craft field showed me the possibilities of a career in textiles. Toshiko Takaezu, famed ceramicist, and Lenore Tawney, touted as the grandmother of contemporary fibers, both came to visit me in Guatemala, where I was studying backstrap weaving with a Mayan family. For two weeks we traveled to remote villages, marveling at the intricate and beautiful textiles of the country. It was during this trip that I decided to put my life's energy into the teaching of modern forms of textiles. I spent the next twenty plus years teaching textiles and drawing at Slippery Rock University in Pennsylvania and at Koç University in Istanbul, Turkey. I was also fulfilling a parallel career in commissioned tapestries."

Akiko Kotani, born in Waipahu, Hawaii, studied painting at the University of Hawaii and textiles at the Tyler School of Art. Her work was deeply influenced by the Mayan weaving techniques she learned while living in Guatemala over a two-year period. Kotani's visual sense and training as a painter comes through in her distinctive approach to weaving and embroidery techniques. She first developed the idea of painting with threads in the 1970s and continues this practice today, employing basic colors and simple stitching techniques to convey essential ideas. Her approach is deliberately minimalistic, and her Buddhist practice encompasses the repetitive, meditative process of weaving, embroidering, crocheting, and drawing.

Angela Hennessy

Oakland, California
b. 1971

OPPOSITE
A Chosen Universe,
2021
Synthetic hair, artist's
hair, and twist tie wire;
68 × 48 inches
(173 × 122 cm)

ABOVE LEFT
Night Flowers, 2021
Synthetic hair, artist's
hair, and twist tie wire;
48 × 48 inches
(122 × 122 cm)

ABOVE RIGHT
Bearing, 2021
Synthetic hair, artist's
hair, and twist tie wire;
48 × 48 inches
(122 × 122 cm)

"I grew up in a family of artists: painters, photographers, ceramicists, sewers, quilters, and crocheters. Creative work was always respected and taken seriously. Textiles were central to everyday life. My grandmother was always sewing something, and we often went to fabric stores and planned out projects together. In my work, I am trying to make myself recognizable to my ancestors—I'm trying to communicate with my dead people. Everything I make is in service to them."

As a young person in Northern California, Angela Hennessy tried to understand her hair as part of her origin, something she later understood as a main signifier of racialized identity, along with skin color. In graduate school at the California College of the Arts, while working with black velvet fabric (separating the threads), she noticed that the fluffy texture looked like afro hair. She now primarily works with textiles, crocheting synthetic and human hair to create large-scale sculptures addressing cultural narratives of the body and mortality. In 2015, Hennessy survived a gunshot wound while interrupting a violent assault on the street in front of her house. Following the experience, she wrote her manifesto, "The School of the Dead," which moves between poetry, prayer, and call to action. Hennessy constructs sculptures and installations with everyday domestic labor—washing, wrapping, crocheting, knotting, brushing, and braiding. She volunteers with hospice and works with families on home funerals, death vigils, and grief rituals. She is a professor at the California College of the Arts, and cofounder of the Black feminist movement See Black Womxn.

Anna Wallack

Newburyport, Massachusetts
b. 1977

"My dad had a huge influence on how I think about my work (and everything, really). He encouraged me to trust my instincts and showed me that art and craft are valid and noble pursuits. He taught me how to care for and love clothing (shining shoes and de-pilling sweaters). And he taught me how to thrift, looking for cashmere and 100 percent wool. It was always about materials. Raw materials are pure potential, and they have integrity and value."

Born in Western Massachusetts, Anna Wallack was taught to knit by both of her grandmothers during school vacations in Florida. For a long time, knitting was simply an activity she enjoyed. Then, while on maternity leave from a career as a stylist, Wallack was inspired to start a children's knitwear line. She wanted to create knitted garments that would become meaningful heirlooms. She looked at available patterns but didn't find what she wanted, so she started writing her own and quickly developed a personal catalog. She then launched her brand Misha & Puff. Soon after starting the company, Wallack began a partnership with a community of knitters on the outskirts of Lima, Peru. She wanted her knitted garments to be made ethically and thoughtfully; to source organic, high-quality materials locally; and to endorse a long-standing artisan tradition.

Channing Hansen

Los Angeles, California
b. 1972

"Working with cloth came about through my exploration of materials and through my habit of collecting hobbies. I had already been making performance and sculpture for many years when I took up knitting just to keep my restless hands busy when I was away from the studio. The more I knitted, the more I saw its potential as a medium for art, how it was related to drawing and kinetic sculpture. I also began to recognize how it connected to my interest in the history of science and technology."

Channing Hansen was born in Los Angeles, California, where he continues to live and work. He studied at San Francisco Art Institute as part of its New Genres program, working mostly in performance and video. Around 2008, Hansen began developing a fiber-based art practice as a way to further his interest in science and technology. He collects, processes, and dyes raw fleece from conservation-bred sheep. After spinning fleece into yarn, Hansen transforms the material into complex forms through knitting and weaving.

Elaborate computer algorithms dictate his designs, combining craft and computation. In uniting technology with man-made and environmental concerns, Hansen's work underscores our interconnected place in the universe—whether to the earth itself, an algorithmic world, or the cosmos—and asks us to consider what mark we should leave behind. His large hand-knitted textiles are mounted on wooden stretchers and feature vibrant, abstract forms that undulate across their weblike surfaces.

Daphne Chen

Portland, Oregon
b. 1997

"As a young child, I was interested in what cloth could become. I was always enamored with the costumes I was surrounded by and the overall clothing itself. The costumes transformed people and gave them a new identity. Additionally, thinking back, I've always also been attracted to the way the light hits the fabric; the colors come alive, and the fabric sparkles and moves with each person."

As a child in New York City, Daphne Chen was involved in theater, which exposed her early on to fabric adorned with beading, sequins, and trims. She studied textiles at the Rhode Island School of Design, and during her freshman year she realized the complexity and diversity of cloth. Her friends encouraged her to explore textiles further, and she cites them as her biggest supporters. Chen's passions grew for structural investigations of dimensionality in knitting and weaving. Using the Stoll M1plus pattern software, Chen used her knowledge of knitting to investigate different variations of knit structure combinations to create three-dimensional fabrics. Her work experiments with how color, material, and structure can evoke a visceral experience of relationships and environments. She is passionate about programming and working with the industrial Jacquard loom and the Stoll machine, and her work revolves around dimensionality, identity, and creating narratives.

Debra Weiss

Los Angeles, California
b. 1956

"Since I was a child I have loved textiles. I learned to sew and crochet from my mom. I loved to play with color and texture and manipulate things with my hands. I taught myself macramé and followed my instinct at fifteen to be an entrepreneur and make things to sell as I challenged myself to learn new techniques. My mom was my initial teacher, but I believe it was my excitement for creating and improvising that pushed me farther along the path to where I am today. From my experience, I have been able to encourage my daughters to seek and follow their passion."

Debra Weiss was born in Los Angeles, just half a mile from where she lives now. As a child she made clothes, blankets, and curtains for herself and for her dolls. Growing up in the 1960s, she saw sewing and crocheting as a practical tool and craft, rather than as art. In college Weiss studied science and textile design. Needing to make a living, she ended up working in the medical field for twenty-five years. During those years, she was always making and creating, while also raising her three daughters. She never stopped working with fiber, embroidering, piecing, stitching, knotting, crocheting, and weaving. In 2000, Weiss started a business designing clothes, Specks & Keepings, which is always evolving. Her pieces have become more art focused recently, and they relay messages about years of life experiences through layers of fabric. The soft and supple quality of textiles has always moved her.

ektor garcia

Nomadic
b. 1985

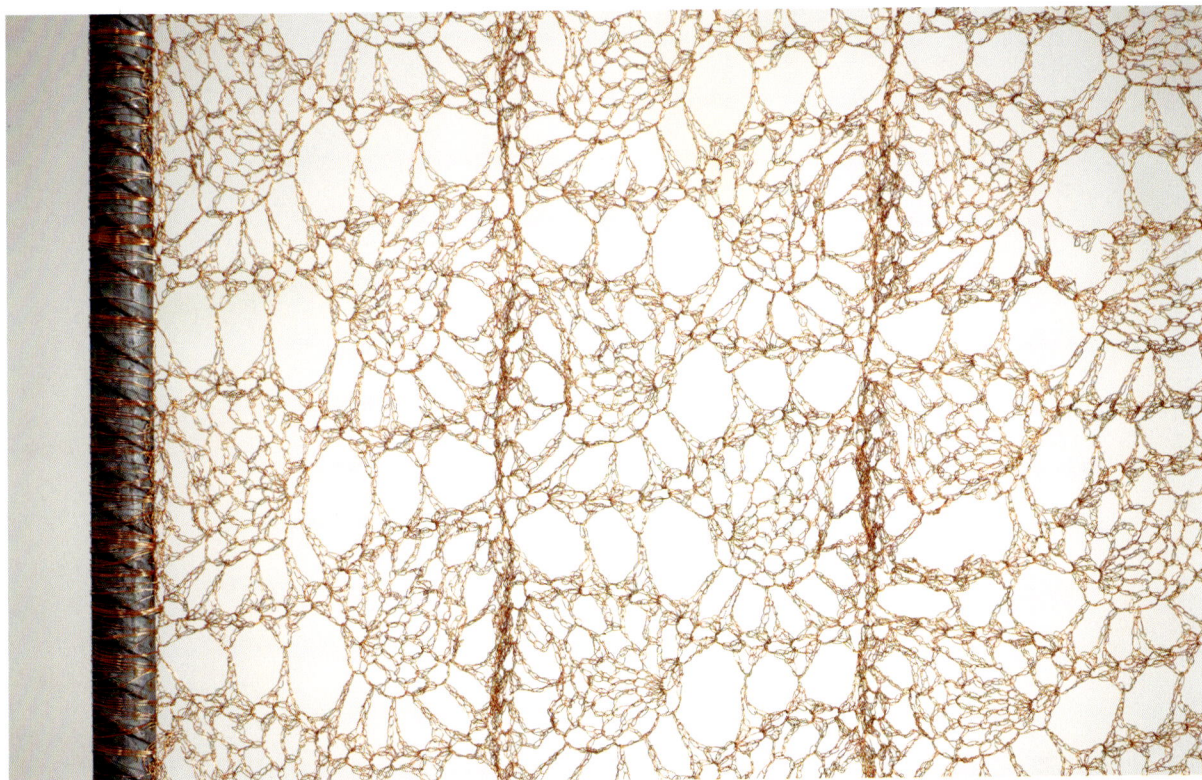

OPPOSITE
Portal Monarcas,
2022
Crocheted copper
wire; 93 × 32 inches
(236 × 81 cm)

ABOVE
Portal III, 2019/2022
(detail)
Crocheted copper
wire, copper,
welded steel;
73 × 52 × 17 inches
(187 × 132 × 43 cm)

"My maternal grandmother would crochet blankets, clothing, and doilies for the house and for her many children, grandchildren, and great-grandkids. My grandfather used to work making all kinds of baskets when he was young, and he recently started making them again. There is an independent, self-sufficient nature in the way my family repairs and creates things, out of necessity— working with what was at hand and materials that could be upcycled."

Born in Red Bluff, California, ektor garcia remembers his grandmother crocheting doilies. As a teenager (and in his early twenties) garcia saw punk kids hand-sewing patches onto their clothes with dental floss and making experimental crocheted clothing. He realized then that crochet could be used to make things beyond doilies and blankets, and he started crocheting unconventional masks and outfits. garcia received his BFA from the School of the Art Institute of Chicago in 2014, and his MFA from Columbia University in New York in 2016.

He garnered positive feedback and encouragement from peers and professors while in undergrad, and he cites the Fiber Material Studies department as essential to his formation as a textile artist. Over the years his crochet work has evolved to sculptural (freestanding and hanging) pieces. Across his artistic practice, garcia challenges the hierarchies of gendered and racialized labor, combining a queer punk sensibility with the handcraft traditions of Mexico, his ancestral homeland. garcia lives and works nomadically.

Emily Holtzman

Cambridge, Massachusetts
b. 1996

OPPOSITE AND ABOVE
Flat knitting machine swatches

"My maternal grandmother, Mary Jane Sexton (and her mother, Jane Calkins), sewed curtains, cushions, napkins, and tablecloths to make her house a home. I now have all of her thimbles and a tomato pin cushion. My great-aunt Kathleen Alger knits and crochets scarves and blankets for our family and for newborns at her church. And my great-grandmother on my father's side, Gwendolyn Temple, was an avid knitter. She lived to be 102."

Growing up in Albany, New York, Emily Holtzman loved to draw and paint. She wasn't aware of textiles as a medium until attending the Rhode Island School of Design. She planned to study illustration and painting but changed course when she saw the textile equipment. She was particularly drawn to a vintage knitting machine that looked like "a cross between a keyboard piano and the back of a deep-sea fishing boat." She found a true passion for industrial knitting and Jacquard weaving and received a BFA in Textiles in 2018. Her explorations in textile structure are made on Jacquard looms, hand flat knitting machines, and industrial knitting machines. Now a textile engineer at MIT's Lincoln Laboratory, Holtzman works on a variety of research and design projects that range from knitting biomedical textiles to integrating microelectronics into fabrics through techniques including knitting, weaving, and technical embroidery. She is happiest at work when she is programming and knitting structures on the Stoll Autarkic Direct Feed machine (*autarkic* meaning "independent" in German).

Emily Nora O'Neil

Portland, Maine
b. 1989

OPPOSITE
Immortelle Lace,
2020
Knit cotton and
raw silk

ABOVE
Rosa Rugosa Lace,
2021
Knit cotton and
raw silk

"I fell in love with a technique known as stranded color work. Using graph paper and a punch card, I draft repeating patterns that in essence become lace when knit with two contrasting weights of yarn. I particularly love working with heavier cotton and delicate raw silk.

"When I was in college my mom gifted me a book on the history of swimwear that I treasure as references to silhouettes. I frequently circle back to ask myself if what I am doing feels honest and not overworked."

Emily Nora O'Neil was born where the mountains meet the sea in Rockport, Maine. Creating has always been instinctual for her, a language she has used to connect with others and interpret the world around her. Her mother, a seamstress and mural painter, has been an example for a creative life. Sensitive to how things look and feel, O'Neil had an appreciation for textiles early on, but she didn't understand it as a medium to explore professionally until attending art school at the Rhode Island School of Design. O'Neil connected quickly to knitting because of the opportunity to create objects that others could touch and live with. She works with a hand-operated knitting machine and shapes the knitted cloth into silhouettes to be worn. She is drawn to the intimacy of creating transparent fabrics for the figure. O'Neil teaches at the Maine College of Art and Design and the Rhode Island School of Design.

Jennifer Berg

Albuquerque, New Mexico
b. 1992

OPPOSITE
Various knit patterns
Worsted-weight wool

ABOVE
Sheep Camp
Worsted-weight wool

"I feel like knitwear found me. I was in my second year of college, looking for a way to make gifts for my friends and family. I crocheted before finding knitting and fell in love with it. Using fiber always felt like a way to connect to my roots. Navajo people are known for their beautiful and intricate weavings. We take so much pride in using our weavings for storytelling and connection to who we are. When I was about seven, my grandmothers set up a weaving space to teach all of my cousins, my sister, and me how to weave. In continuing these traditions, I feel more connected with my culture, and I want others to join me on this journey of keeping it alive."

Jennifer Berg is Navajo (Diné, in her native language). She grew up on the Navajo Nation reservation near the New Mexico/Arizona border. Berg started knitting ten years ago with encouragement from a friend to broaden her craft techniques. She started with basic hats, gained the confidence to read patterns, and then began writing her own knitting patterns. Berg naturally felt drawn to incorporate native designs into the patterns she created. Textiles are an integral part of Navajo artistry and, for Berg, knitting felt like a way to share her culture. She loves working with wool and wool mixtures. She grew up with sheep and enjoys the grit and smell of wool. Additionally, wool holds together differently than other fibers, an asset for the type of colorwork Berg uses. She is using her craft to shed light on a people who are often forgotten or misunderstood, and she is raising her children to know their culture too.

Jessica Switzer Green

Sebastopol, California
b. 1964

OPPOSITE
Molly's Harmony,
2022
Felted wool; 7 × 9 feet
(2.1 × 2.7 m)

LEFT
Pangea, 2022
Felted with natural-
and indigo-dyed wool;
35 × 45 inches
(89 × 114 cm)

"My mother, grandmother, and great-grandmother were all painters; they painted for pleasure. My grandfather was a fine art photographer. There was always a lot of art in my family. My mother and grandmothers had wool blankets, so there's a familiarity of the touch and the smell. I believe in my heart that connecting to [wool-producing] animals is part of my English and Russian ancestry. I know in my DNA to be comfortable with wool.

"Felting is the comingling of fibers, through water and abrasion, or needles. Silk and wool love to be felted. Scales on the fibers combine like a plant vine. Lanolin is an important part too, because it is water-repellent. The Vikings used wool for their sails."

Born in San Francisco, Jessica Switzer Green moved to rural Oregon at age six. Her mother and stepfather were part of a countercultural "back to the land" movement, and Switzer Green grew up with lots of animals coming in and out of the house (but no sheep). She majored in Politics at the University of California, Santa Cruz, and then worked creatively in marketing and public relations for thirty years. When her children were grown, she moved from Marin County (north of San Francisco) to more rural Sebastopol and got her first flock of sheep. She sought out ways to make use of the shorn wool and connected with the nearby fibershed community. She started her company, JG SWITZER. in 2018. To create her felted wool fabric, Switzer Green uses a process she calls "painting with wool"— layering undyed and plant-dyed raw fleece. Next, she runs the layers through a repurposed, industrial dry-felting machine (with 10,000 needles, weighing 7½ tons) to create a new, nonwoven textile. Switzer Green cares deeply about the regenerative powers of natural fibers.

I chose the road less traveled and now I don't know where the hell I am.

BE SOME BODY

Josh Faught

San Francisco, California
b. 1979

OPPOSITE
Wake Me Up When the Big Hand's on the Twelve and the Little Hand Is on the Five, 2014
Handwoven and crocheted, wool, cotton, and hemp, woodburned sign, and badge on hand-dyed linen
36 × 42 inches
(91 × 106 cm)

ABOVE
The Mauve Decade (#1) (detail), 2014
Crocheted and woven hemp, hand dyed wool, black sequins, pins, hand-painted wooden sign, coffee spill (resin), and cedar trellis support
66 inches × 70 inches × 3 feet
(167 × 178 ×8 cm)

"My grandmother was certainly an initial inspiration. She was an avid knitter and embroiderer, and so I grew up with her work around the house. As an adult, I was fortunate to learn from Anne Wilson and Joan Livingstone, two brilliant artists and educators, who really encouraged me to rigorously pursue my work within a fine arts practice."

Josh Faught was born in St. Louis, Missouri. His grandmother taught him how to knit at a young age, and her mother had crocheted exquisite lace. Faught learned how to weave on a traditional floor loom while attending summer camp. After a suburban midwestern upbringing and four years of college (he is a graduate of Oberlin), he moved to New York City and worked at *Nest* magazine. He earned additional degrees in Textiles and Fiber Studies from the Fashion Institute of Technology and the School of the Art Institute of Chicago. Faught mixes textiles with everyday objects and pop-cultural detritus that often feature political slogans and elements of kitsch. His assemblages start with raw fibers that he hand-dyes with organic materials or covers with paint. Faught's labor-intensive sculptures draw on histories of gender and sexual politics, and his art practice explores the ways in which textiles and craft function as a means of mobilization, survival, and support. When his work begins to incorporate multiple material histories at once, he comes back to textiles as a way to think about language, abstraction, and community.

Karen and Marie Potesta

Alameda, California
b. 1975 (Marie), 1976 (Karen)

"We visited our grandmother's small childhood home in the Italian countryside, and it was amazing to see an old knitting machine in the house, from the early 1900s. She lived with nine siblings, and they would knit [by machine] all the sweaters and socks for winter. The town worked on a barter system—she could trade a pair of socks for a basket of eggs. Our grandparents' home in Detroit had a sewing room filled wall-to-wall with fabric, yarn, and notions of all kinds. They also had an outdoor cobbler studio. Those were our playrooms. From an early age, we were witness to our grandparents working daily with textiles. The whole home brimmed with creativity and constantly smelled of Italian cooking!"

Sisters Karen and Marie Potesta are only fifteen months apart in age. Their Italian grandparents were their earliest influences in fashion and craft. Their grandmother was a formally trained expert dressmaker, and their grandfather was a shoemaker and inventor. Marie earned a bachelor's degree in Fine Art and then a master's degree in Fashion and Knitwear Design from the Academy of Art University. Karen earned a bachelor's degree in Industrial Engineering, then went on to study fashion design and patternmaking at the Fashion Institute of Design & Merchandising in Los Angeles. Karen and Marie came together to launch their knitwear label, Micaela Greg. Their knitwear is made in California, New York, and Peru and is constructed of the finest-quality yarns. They collaborate closely with knitters and seamstresses, supporting local industries and art forms.

Kristina Foley

McMinnville, Oregon
b. 1983

"The head of the Fiber Arts program at Syracuse University, Ann Clarke, played a pivotal role in connecting me with artists who were exploring the intersections of textiles, fashion, and art with other fields. Now my professional path emphasizes weaving together my love of natural fibers, botanical color, sustainability, and innovation with rebuilding a healthy agricultural and textile industry in the United States."

Kristina Foley participated in a Waldorf homeschool community as a child, and her mother encouraged a love of plants and textiles. Her great-grandmother immigrated to New York with only her sewing machine to support herself. Foley was introduced to felting wool while completing a BFA in Fiber Structure and Interlocking at Syracuse University and continued her practice after graduation, when she moved to Italy. In Tuscany, she developed a "nomadic studio" that reflected the local materials available: European wool varieties, dye plants, and secondhand textiles. Her professional work in fashion and design, while immersed in the artisan culture of Florence, was influential to her craft. In 2018, Kristina moved to Oregon and created Basic Needs, small collections intertwining beauty, utility, and sustainability. Her felted sheepskins highlight the incredible wool available from small farms in the Pacific Northwest.

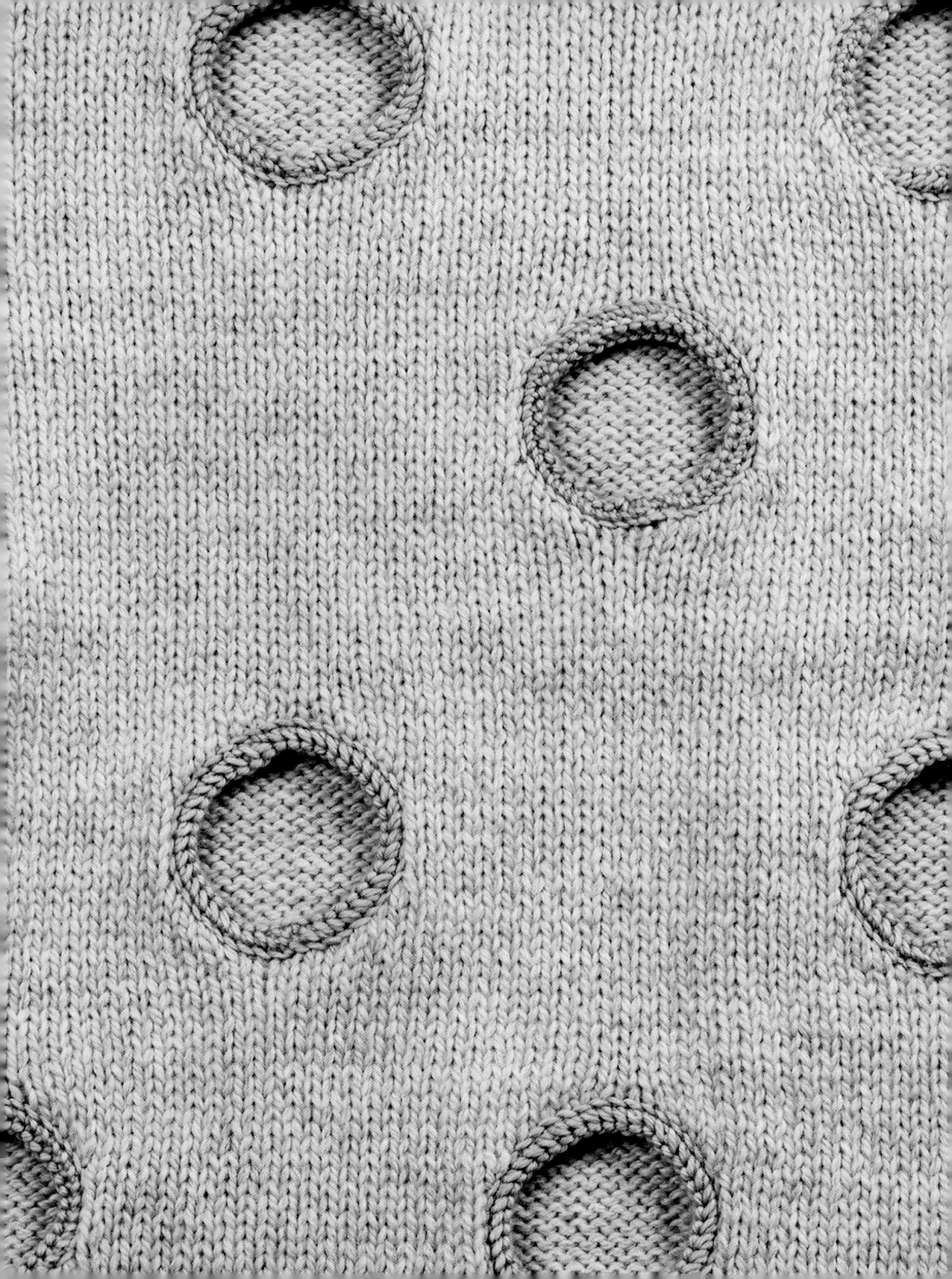

Lindsay Degen

Providence, Rhode Island
b. 1988

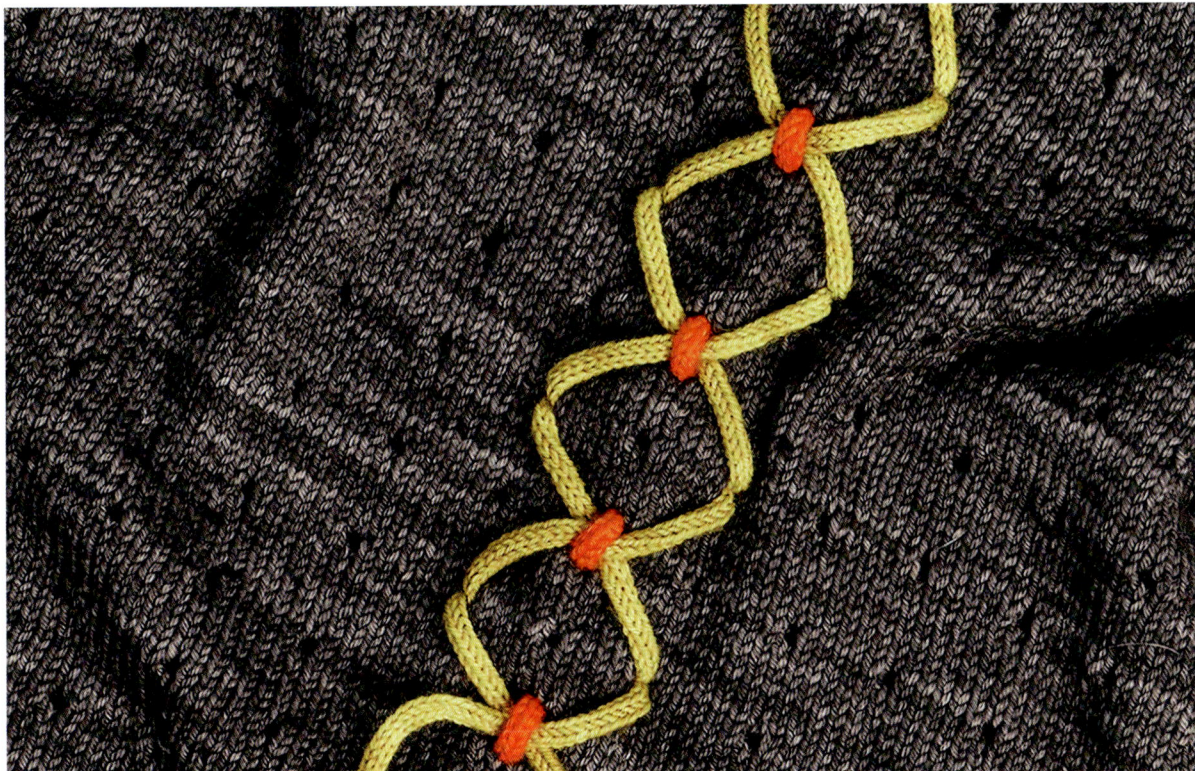

OPPOSITE
Hole Sweater
Highland wool,
Stockinette knit
stitch with crocheted
holes

ABOVE
*LYOA Sweater (Lace
Your Own Adventure)*
Merino wool,
Stockinette stitch
with pointelle in a grid

"Both of my parents are scientists, but my mom sews and is an avid cross-stitcher. My parents have done a lot of traveling and collecting of local folk arts and crafts. I think my love of tactility came from all of the multicultural artifacts I grew up around: wooden masks, intricately engraved nutshells, teapots, a boomerang, a painting made of colored sand. This wasn't specifically cloth, but I was exposed generally to tactile pieces made by artisans from around the world."

Born in Cincinnati, Ohio, Lindsay Degen started knitting when she was three, taught by her grandmother. She was always a fidgeter, so having something to keep her hands busy was helpful. Degen attended the Rhode Island School of Design and Central Saint Martins in London. She identifies as a maker, and she started her craft-centered brand DEGEN in 2010. She makes garments slowly and by hand—an intentional practice to ensure ethical and sustainable manufacturing and a high level of craft. Almost a decade ago, Degen began hand-piecing and quilting, balancing her love of knitting with a new ability to explore color and texture in a larger format. Quilting allows Degen to be freer with color compared to knitting (knitting being more rigid with how colorwork is done). Recently, Degen started a knitting community called KNIT.club where knitters gather and knitters of all levels are welcome.

Melissa Dadourian

Brooklyn, New York, and Woodstock, New York
b. 1969

OPPOSITE
Soft Geometry No. 1
(detail), 2023
Hand- and machine-
knitted thread

LEFT
Soft Weirdo, 2023
Hand- and machine-
knitted thread

"My true passion is for material and its embedded history. I use a vintage analog knitting machine to create my woven paintings, which is a time-consuming process. This 'labor' combined with all the decision-making about color, texture, and pattern resonates with who I am as an artist. My grandparents were genocide survivors who escaped what was, at the time, Armenia in 1913. The comfort and history hand-woven textiles offer have informed and influenced my work. It has become a part of my visual language."

Melissa Dadourian is Armenian American and was born in Cleveland, Ohio. She grew up surrounded by imagery and patterns found in carpets, paintings, and various textiles that are now ingrained in her psyche. She studied art, with a focus on painting, at Pratt Institute, then combined media (installation and sculpture) at Hunter College. Dadourian began machine knitting during a residency at the Textile Arts Center in Brooklyn. Her work now intersects painting, object making, and immersive installation. She uses various materials: vintage threads, hand-dyed fabrics, burlap, canvas, paint, and repurposed curtains. Dadourian alters the individual materials with stain, paint, cutting, and sewing, making new patterns and textures on the surfaces of found fabrics. Through shape, color, and texture (and in tandem with beauty, humor, and decoration) she explores her fascination with domesticity, and contradictions coexist in the tension: soft and firm, loose and tight, masculine and feminine. Dadourian pushes the boundaries of what a painting can be.

Micah Clasper-Torch

Los Angeles, California
b. 1986

"Working with textiles has been a lifelong calling, beginning as an interest in fashion and interior design. I realized the power that cloth had and the myriad of ways it could be transformed and incorporated into our lives. Growing up with hand-me-down clothing and shopping at Goodwill, I learned how to recognize quality fabric and understand the value of natural materials over synthetic. I love natural fibers, texture, discarded or upcycled materials, and fabric that has been manipulated or decorated by hand. Textiles have such life in them."

Micah Clasper-Torch was born in Dayton, Ohio, and raised in Providence, Rhode Island, by parents who encouraged her creativity and artistic exploration. She studied at the Fashion Institute of Technology in New York and the Politecnico di Milano in Italy. For fifteen years she worked in the realms of fashion, art, and design. In 2018 she created her first punch needle coat, combining her background in tailoring and her interest in the underrepresented technique of punch needle hooking. The following year, she trained and was formally certified as an Oxford punch needle instructor by Amy Oxford, renowned rug hooker and founder of the Oxford Rug Hooking School in Vermont. In 2020, Clasper-Torch launched Punch Needle World, an online community and educational platform dedicated to the art, craft, and history of punch needle rug hooking. Her work embraces traditional craft traditions while exploring new techniques and applications.

Pauline Shaw

Brooklyn, New York
b. 1988

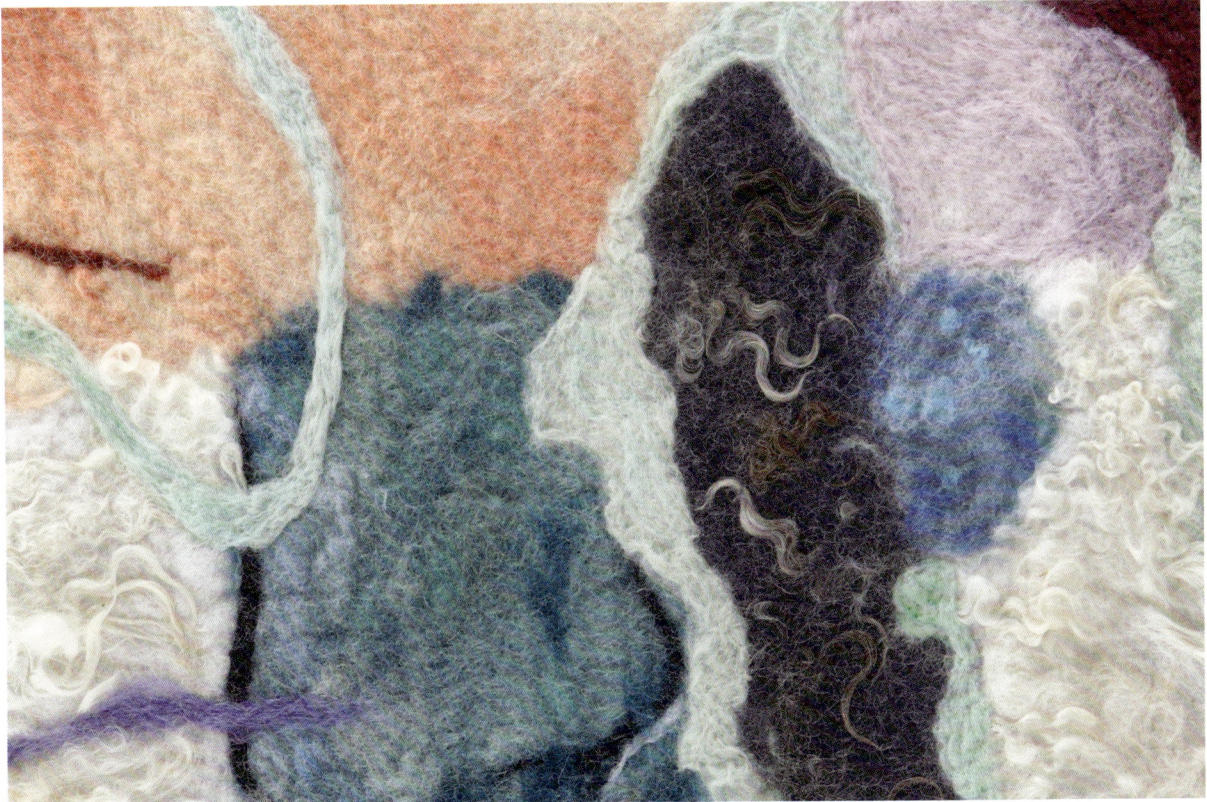

"My grandparents owned a textile factory in Taiwan. It wasn't until after I began felting and working with textiles that I learned more about it and went back to visit the old factory (which is now owned by a distant uncle and is defunct). It was really interesting to visit the town that my grandparents and parents are from and see the old factory with all the machines—now sitting in darkness."

Pauline Shaw is Taiwanese American and was born in Kirkland, Washington. As a child she always enjoyed working creatively with her hands. She received her BFA from the Rhode Island School of Design in 2011, and her MFA at Columbia University in 2019. Shaw describes a continued interest in learning new techniques that led her to experiment with felting. She experienced a fascination with the alchemy of the process and the fiber— including going to a granular level to understand dyeing, pH levels, and the hardness of the cloth. In her large-scale felted panes and multimedia sculpture work, Shaw examines historical and modern representations of self-identity and lineage. She meditates on the relationships between body and spirit, cultural and ancestral history, and science and mysticism. As a first-generation Asian American woman, she has observed the erasure of traditions, mythologies, and memories. Through her work, she communicates the rootlessness and cultural confusion of a diasporic and immigrant experience.

Rose Pearlman

Brooklyn, New York
b. 1979

OPPOSITE AND ABOVE
Punch needle–hooked wool on linen

"When my mother had young children to care for and a full-time job, she could no longer devote the time and space needed to paint with oil. She taught herself to hook rugs with simple supplies and common materials so that her paintings could easily be reimagined in wool. In this way, she could slowly chip away at a large floor rug in the presence of family, in a home setting, and in what small free time she had. In-process rugs in large frames would lean against the wall, baskets of fiber tucked away next to the sofa, ready for whenever my mother had a moment to spare. With my mother as an example, I've maintained a creative practice despite the time and space limitations."

Rose Pearlman grew up in a creative home; her mother is an abstract painter and made hooked rugs in their living room. Prior to picking up a punch needle herself, Pearlman was a teaching artist in New York City public schools and museums. Her focus was on the visual arts, centered around a curriculum of world cultures. In her early thirties, with a new baby, Pearlman decided to try hooking, and she found it creative, convenient, and soothing. Hooking rugs uses the artistic vocabulary of color and form and is also a medium that provides utility and comfort. Pearlman realized the versatility of the craft would keep her interested, and the freedom of expression would challenge and push her to grow as an artist. Her work blurs the lines between art and craft and pushes the boundaries with nontraditional techniques and materials. She is the author of *Modern Rug Hooking* and coauthor of *Making Things*.

Sagarika Sundaram

Manhattan, New York
b. 1986

"Most people from Southern India have an innate relationship with handloom fabric because there's so much of it every day. I am thinking about my mother's saris and my father's vesh-tis. Wearing these garments requires a literacy with pleating and folding cloth. I can picture my grandmother washing her nine-yard sari in our apartment in Chennai (Madras). She would fold the cloth precisely, throw it over a clothesline hung high up with a long stick, and use the tool to methodically unfold it out to dry.

"With art, nobody's asking me to do this work; there's no client. Art is the truest mirror of my subconscious self. It's much more ambiguous what that end result will be, and I find great joy in that journey. I want to be very playful in my work and my life. Working in this way connects me to myself, to my inner world."

Sagarika Sundaram was born in Kolkata, India, and grew up between India and Dubai. At age eleven she attended the Rishi Valley boarding school. Sundaram describes the school as having a spirit of inquiry, where students could question and challenge their teachers. Many of her classmates' parents were artists. She learned dyeing and batik, and began to think about textiles as art. She went to college in the United States, at Parsons/The New School in New York, and the Maryland Institute College of Art in Baltimore. After eight years working in corporate design, she pivoted to work as a full-time artist. Her large felted installations bind together organic and constructed forms. To start, she mixes her own dye formulations and dyes the sheep wool, which she sources near and far (from Upstate New York to the Himalayas). She then lays the wool down (like sketching), and the fibers felt with the application of water and friction. Sundaram is a visiting assistant professor at Pratt Institute and a senior fellow at Silver Art Projects in New York City.

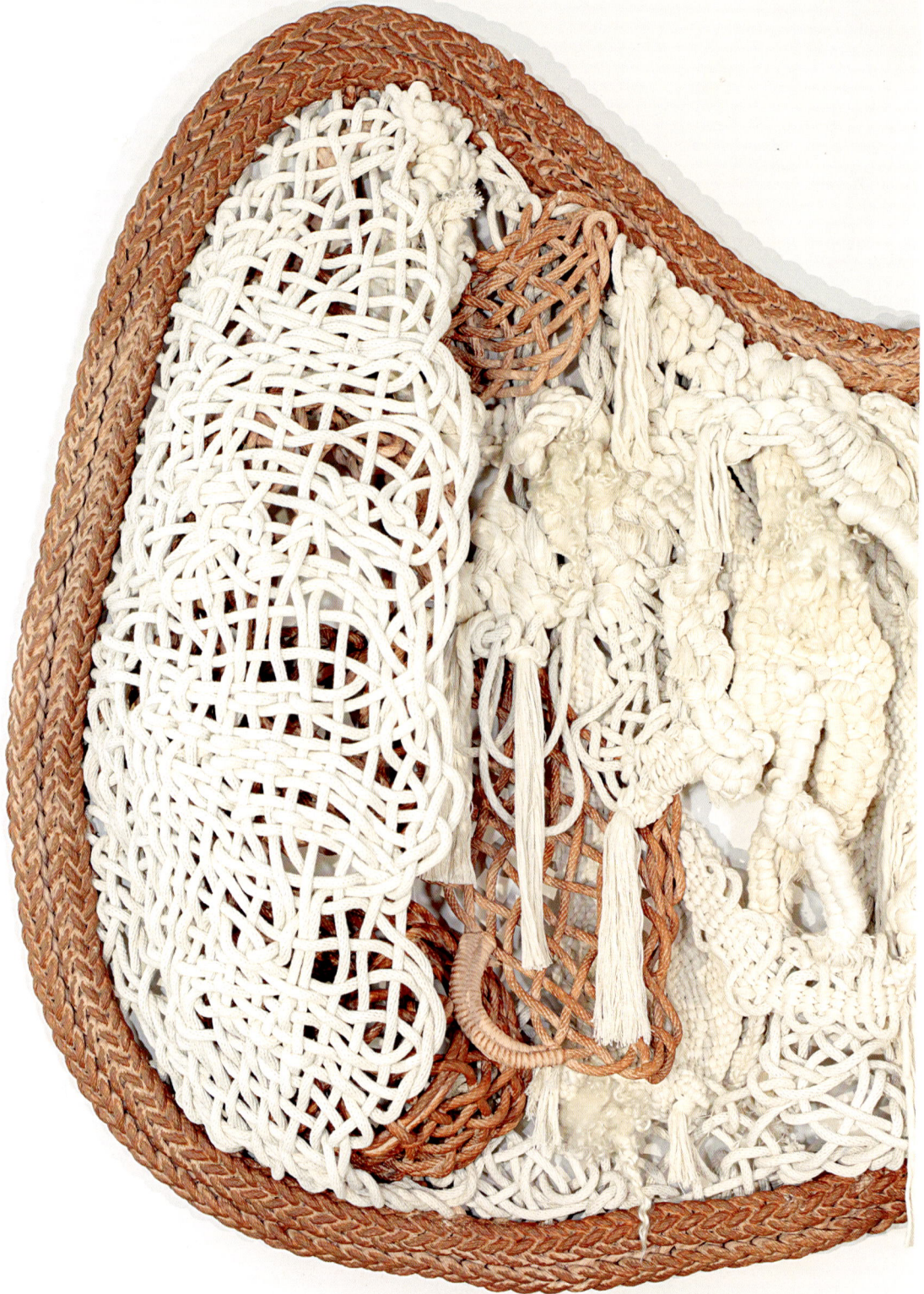

Tanya Aguiñiga

Los Angeles, California
b. 1978

"Having educators I could relate to in my struggles with identity helped me flip a switch that led me to where I am now. Art gave me power. For a lot of us who are marginalized or seen as others, art can explore different ways of telling our stories. Learning about fiber, fabric, and textiles can help you take ownership of how you present yourself to the world. Once you learn how to make your own fabric, your own clothes, you will be more self-sufficient but also have authorship of self."

Tanya Aguiñiga was born in San Diego, California, and raised in Tijuana, Mexico. She studied at San Diego State University and then received an MFA in Furniture Design from the Rhode Island School of Design. At RISD she studied under artist Wendy Maruyama, who challenged the masculine environments within the field of woodworking and was one of the first women to obtain a master's degree in Furniture Design. Drawing on her upbringing as a binational citizen, Aguiñiga speaks about her experience of her divided identity and aspires to tell the larger and often invisible stories of

the transnational community. Aguiñiga began her career by creating collaborative installations with the Border Art Workshop/Taller de Arte Fronterizo, an artist collective that addressed political and human rights issues at the United States and Mexico border. Aguiñiga works with cotton, wool, and other textiles, drawing upon Mesoamerican weaving and traditional forms. In 2016, in response to the deep polarization about the border, Aguiñiga created AMBOS (Art Made Between Opposite Sides), an ongoing series of projects that provides a platform for binational artists.

Tracy Krumm

Saint Paul, Minnesota
b. 1963

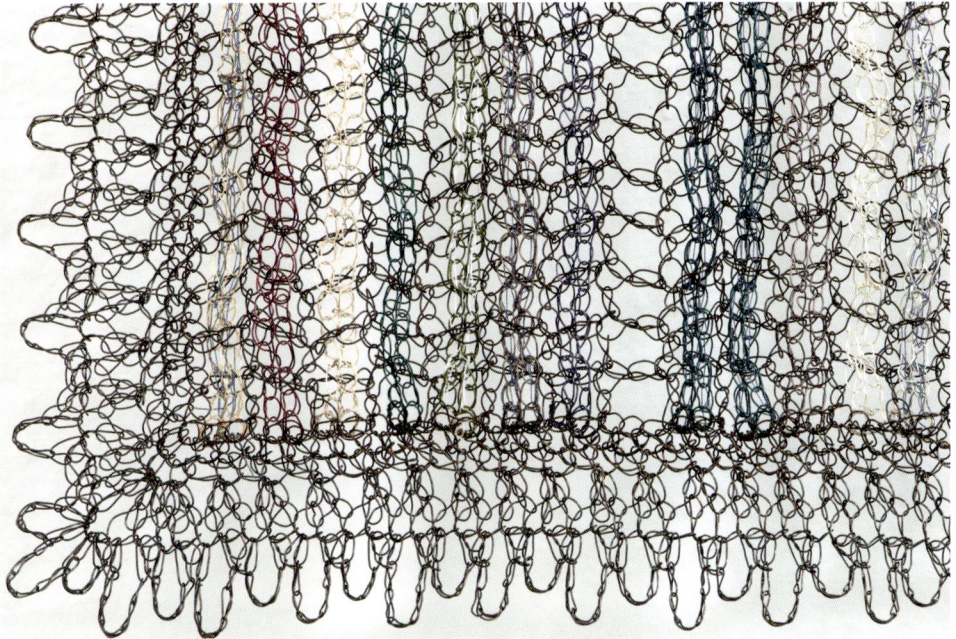

"As a student of cloth, as an educator about cloth, as an artist with a creative practice based in cloth—this all started generations before me. Whenever we visited our elders, handwork was part of their daily routines. In order to spend time with them, we watched and learned. My great-grandmothers were quilters, their mothers were quilters; one grandmother tatted. I can still hear her tell me, 'Over and through, under and through,' as I sat on her lap. Both of my grandmothers crocheted. Great-aunties sewed and knitted. All of the women did embroidery. We learned to mend and repair. I grew up with preservation of skill and the understanding of cloth being an inherent part of life."

Tracy Krumm's first forays into knitting and crochet were at age six or seven. Born in Kenosha, Wisconsin, she grew this early love of craft to include weaving, beadwork, and sewing. She didn't know then that textiles and fiber art could be a professional pursuit. Krumm had the opportunity to study visual design and craftsmanship with Gail Tremblay at the Evergreen State College, and Tremblay encouraged Krumm's weaving skills. Via Tremblay, Krumm learned about the textile program at the California College of the Arts and moved to the Bay Area to

attend, receiving her BFA. Continuing her studies, she later earned an MFA in Visual Art from Vermont College of Fine Arts. Krumm loves science and math. Through intensive and intricate construction, her work often undertakes a computational, building-block approach where parts and pieces are planned and systematized. At other times, her practice is random and messy, where colors, patterns, and forms develop organically. She is director of artistic advancement at the Textile Center in Minneapolis and maintains her studio practice in Saint Paul.

Trish Andersen

Savannah, Georgia
b. 1984

"I feel very fortunate that my family nurtured and supported my creativity from an early age. I've had a winding road, and yet my parents have always been champions for my work (even if they didn't understand what I was doing). And my grandmother loved cloth; her home was dripping with the most beautiful textiles and patterns. I remember the pattern on her sofa. I wish she could see what I am doing now."

Trish Andersen grew up in Dalton, Georgia, a city nicknamed "Carpet Capital of the World." Wall-to-wall tufted carpet was first produced there, and much of it still is today. Andersen's family manufactured doormats, and she grew up watching the industrial machines and climbing on giant rolls of carpet. Andersen always loved using her hands, and she knew, from a young age, that she wanted to be an artist. She attended the Savannah College of Art and Design and explored lots of different mediums, including painting and ceramics. After college she moved to Brooklyn, where she established a design studio specializing in large-scale installations for events and interiors. Andersen continued that work for thirteen years, eventually leading to burnout; she made the choice to get back into creating art again. She rediscovered tufting and was hooked; it was a means to express her art and connect with her family roots. The tool she primarily uses is a tufting gun, differing from the machine tufting in Dalton. The tool allows her to jump around the frame and work intuitively, like painting. She created Trish Andersen Studio in 2018 and has her hands in both the fine art and home textile/product worlds.

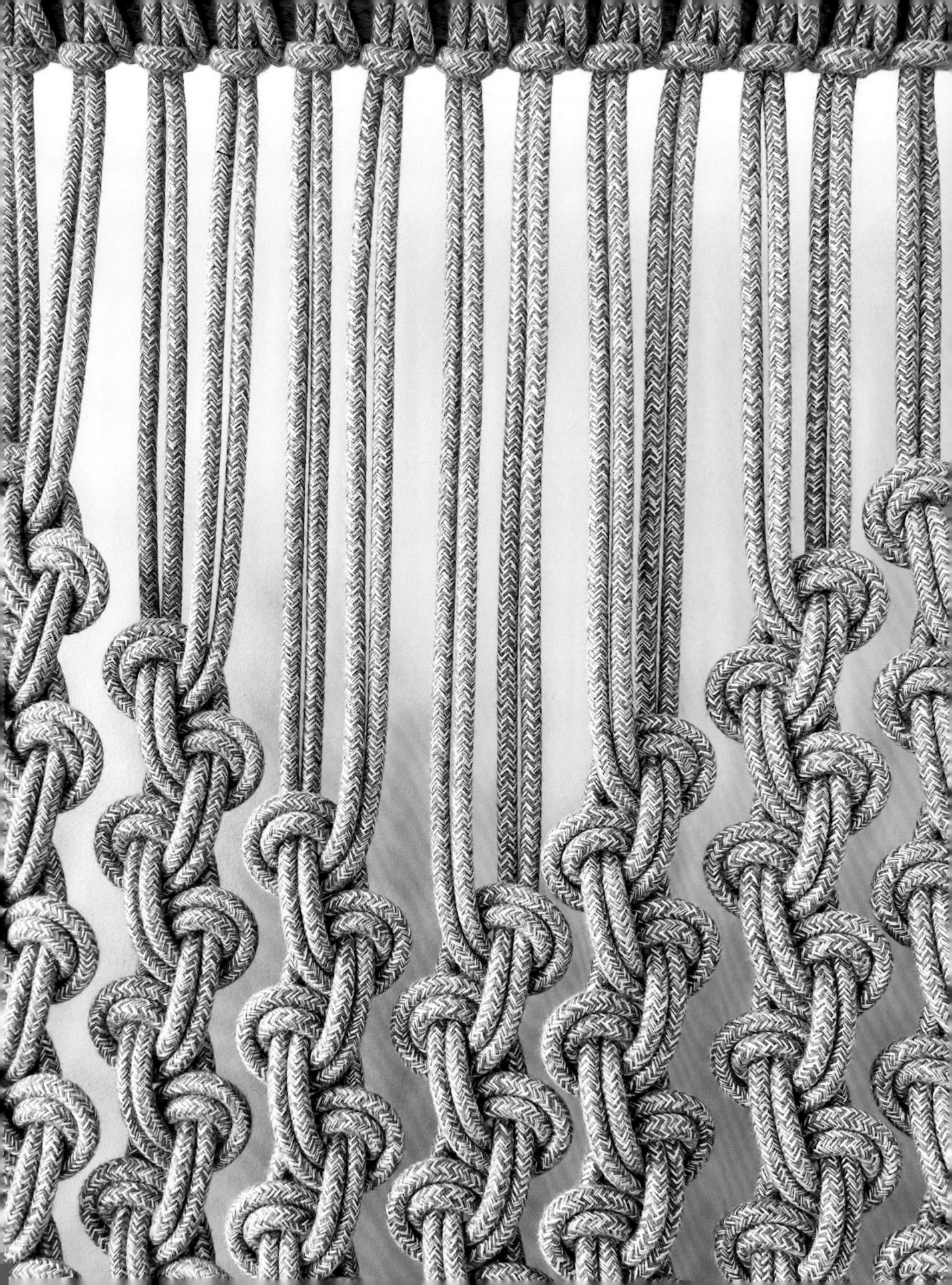

Windy Chien

San Francisco, California
b. 1967

OPPOSITE
Linescape, 2023 (detail)
Sunbrella cordage, walnut;
56 × 81 × 2 inches
(142 × 206 × 5 cm)

ABOVE
Bridge Linescape, 2020 (detail)
Sunbrella cordage, walnut;
48 × 96 × 2 inches
(122 × 244 × 5 cm)

"My grandmother was the only other artist in my family, and during the evenings and weekends, she created a body of work consisting of many dozens of pieces of petit point (a form of fine needlepoint). When her eyesight declined, she stopped making representational works and simply drew random colors from her thread basket to create stunning geometric abstractions without preconceived compositions in mind. Winifred has passed, but I have all her work."

Windy Chien was born in Taipei, Taiwan, and moved to the United States as an infant. Because her father was in the army, her family moved often; they lived in Georgia, Washington, Colorado, Beijing, Hawaii, and New York state. In the 1970s, Chien's mother taught her macramé, the art of square knotting. She made a plant hanger and loved it. In 1989, Chien attended college at California State University in San Francisco, majoring in Film Production. Her undergraduate thesis film screened at the 1994 Sundance Film Festival. For fourteen years, she owned the internationally renowned music shop Aquarius Records.

Chien then had great success in the music industry and at Apple Inc., where she worked on iTunes, iBooks, podcasts, and movies as an editor, consultant, and product manager. After leaving her corporate job at Apple, she aimed to live a life prioritizing her personal creativity. She found knotting again and fell in love with the practice. In 2016 she began a project of learning a new knot every day for a year. Chien's book, *The Year of Knots*, was published by Abrams in 2019. She shares the same name as her grandmother Winifred Chien, who fled China for Taiwan in 1949 after the fall of Chiang Kai-shek's government.

Wet Felting Swatches

Felting is a process of creating cloth by combining and compressing individual fibers, traditionally from the wool coat of animals like sheep, goats, yak, and rabbits. Brightly colored felt sheets used in children's art projects are machine-produced with synthetic fibers. Natural felt is made in one of two basic ways: wet or dry felting. Wet felting by hand (agitating the fibers enough to bind them) takes some physical strength! I find this process to be very playful, and I enjoy how different it is from other methods of making cloth.

MATERIALS

Bath towel

Bubble wrap (with small bubbles) approximately 12 inches (30.5 cm) wide and 4 feet (1.2 m) long

Wool roving in several colors

Spray bottle filled with water

Dish or hand soap

Rolling pin

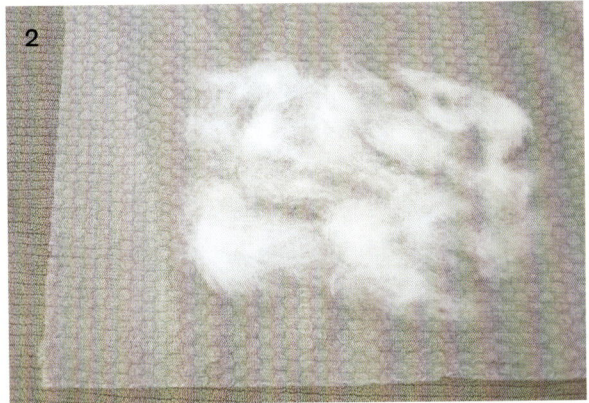

NOTE: *Wet felting appeals to me because of its lack of rigidity and free-form nature (something I'm always trying to exercise in myself). Similar to dyeing, wet felting has elements of control, like choosing colors and placement, but (even for an expert) the final results are always somewhat a surprise.*

INSTRUCTIONS

1. Place a towel on your work surface. On top of the towel, place the bubble wrap, bubble side up. Work at one end of the bubble wrap, leaving the remainder to be folded back over the wool.

2. Find the end of a roving ball and spread apart the fibers. Pull off small portions of wool from the ball, as if you were pulling off a piece of cotton candy. Lay the pieces down, slightly overlapping horizontally in a rectangle shape approximately 6 × 9 inches (15 × 23 cm).

3. Create a second layer, with pieces of wool facing vertically. Depending on your desired thickness, stop here.

4. To create a thicker felted piece, continue layering wool roving, horizontally and vertically.

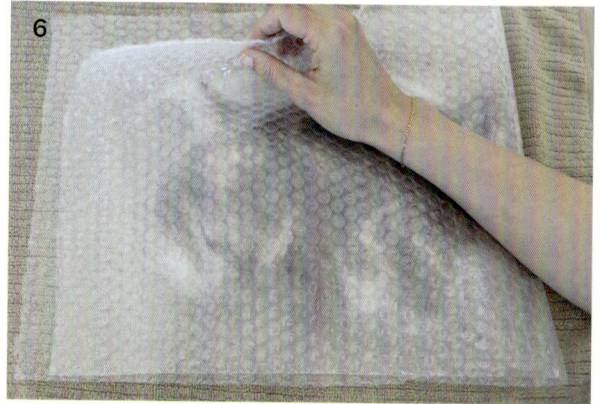

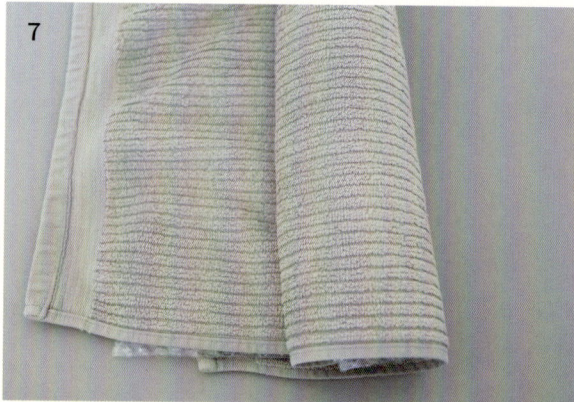

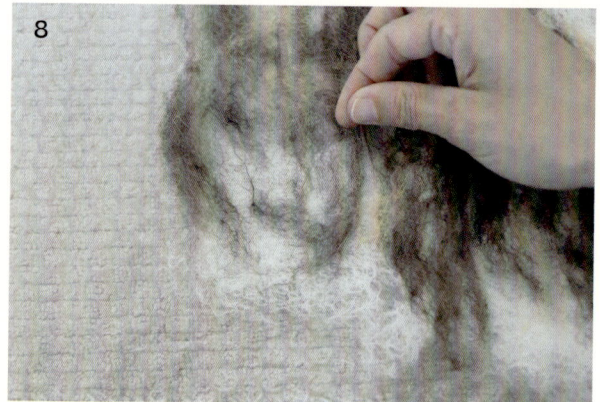

5. Spray the wool until it's moderately wet. Squeeze soap to cover your palms and gently apply soap to the wool.

6. Cover the wool with bubble wrap by folding over the unused portion of bubble wrap, bubble side down.

7. At one end, use the rolling pin to roll the towel, bubble wrap, and wool into a tube. Roll back and forth forty times, gently at first, then gradually increase pressure. Rotate and flip the wool bundle, and roll from every direction.

8. Open up the bubble wrap to check the wool. A pinch test will show whether the wool fibers have felted into a piece of cloth. If the roving fibers lift easily, more rolling/agitating is needed. When the wool has felted to your satisfaction, wash the felted wool in water to remove the soap. Lay the wool in a warm spot to dry completely.

Crochet with Plastic Bags

Similar to T-shirt weaving, this project makes use of an item we have in excess. Many cities have banned plastic bags, or charge money for them, and there might be a point when this project won't be possible (let's hope). I won't detail steps for how to crochet here—but, you can find instructions online, in books at the library and elsewhere, or at your local yarn store. Below are directions for how to turn a plastic bag into usable yarn, also nicknamed "plarn." When developing this project, Chloe May Brown and I found that crochet stitches with open gaps were appealing.

MATERIALS

4 to 6 thin plastic grocery bags

Scissors

Crochet hook, US 7/4.5mm (or similar size)

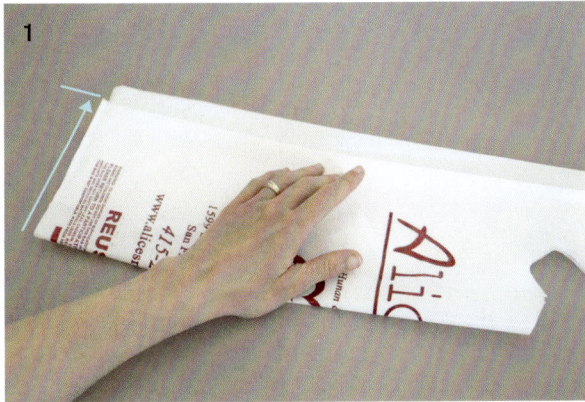

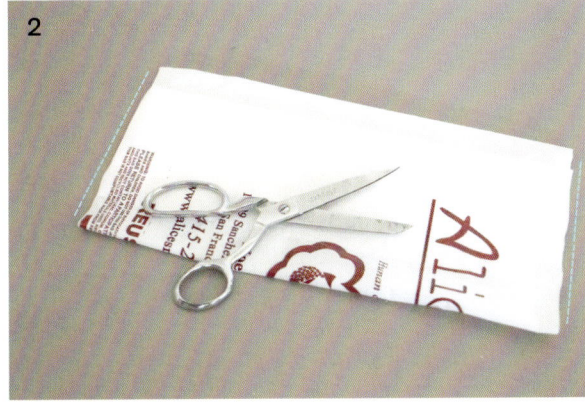

NOTE: *Begin collecting thin plastic bags, possibly from family and friends. Bags with a logo or other printed design will create a nice mottled yarn appearance. When cutting the plastic bags, don't worry if cuts are not perfectly straight; the process is forgiving.*

INSTRUCTIONS

1. Tuck in the gussets of a plastic bag and fold it in half widthwise, save for 1 inch (2.5 cm). (See arrow in Step 1 image for folding distance.)

2. Trim the bag at the top and bottom, removing the handles and the bottom strip.

3. Starting at the folded edge, begin cutting 1-inch-wide (2.5 cm) strips (by eye) from bottom to top, stopping just past the folded edge. Continue along the entire width of the bag.

4. Open up the bag to a single layer, and find the two portions that still connected (appearing like a rib cage, front and back).

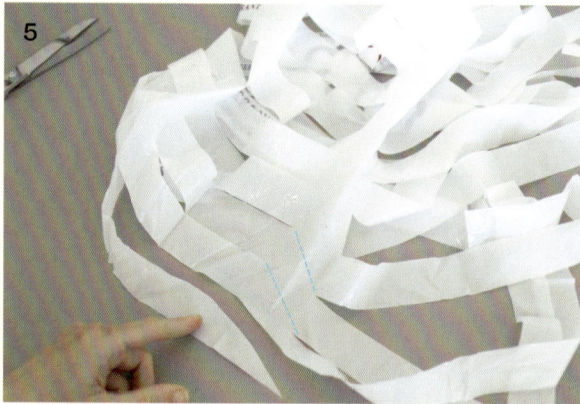

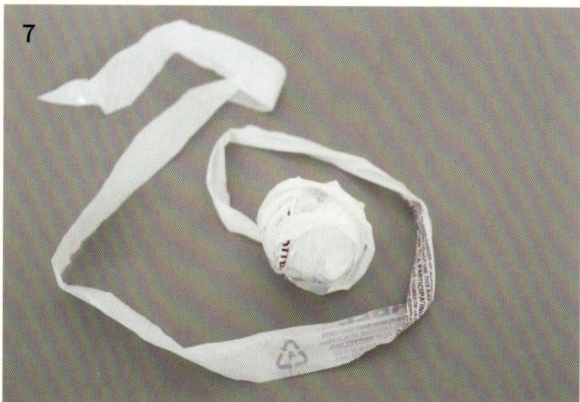

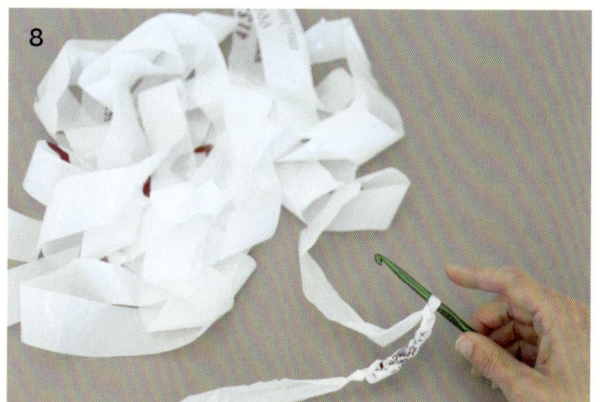

5. For one "rib cage," begin cutting from the end of one slit to the start of another, working diagonally across the uncut space (see photo 5).

6. For the other "rib cage," cut straight across, not diagonally. Trim any odd extra bits of plastic off to smooth the edge.

7. Wind your new plastic yarn into a ball. Repeat steps 1 to 7 with a second plastic bag. Continue with more, as desired.

8. Begin crocheting! The samples shown include Diamond Mesh, Treble Mesh, Open Check, and Honeycomb stitches.

Print and Dye

Making Marks

PRINTING employs tools like wooden blocks, stencils, engraved plates, silk screens, or rollers to embellish cloth. These techniques can be done in an artist's studio at small scale, or in a factory for large production runs. Block (or relief) printing can be done with a variety of materials—from wooden blocks, linoleum, and foam to rubber stamps—and usually involves carving into the block material, then printing an impression of the carved surface with ink. Block printing has a distinctive look that's soft around the edges. Screen printing is a technique for creating a pattern by forcing ink onto a surface through a screen of fine material (silk mesh). Areas of the mesh are blocked out using a liquid filler that dries and becomes a stencil.

Printing Traditions

Wood-block printing is considered one of the original methods used for transferring repeating designs onto cloth, and the earliest surviving examples date from China before 220 CE. Block printing is still widely used on textiles throughout East Asia. *Ajarakh* cloth is hand-carved wood-block-printed fabric made in India and Pakistan. *Kapa* is the traditional Hawaiian bark cloth fabric printed with wooden stamps, which was lost as an art for many generations and is practiced today by dedicated artists continuing the tradition. Dalani Tanahy (page 207) talked about the importance she sees in being a kapa teacher and practitioner: "My work and purpose not only support my life but are tied intrinsically to my culture and identity as a Hawaiian. As part of the revival of a once sleeping art, the teaching component is important to help ensure that kapa-making does not leave our hands again."

Screen printing originated in China during the Song dynasty (960–1279 CE) as a way of transferring designs onto cloth, and it made its way to Europe in the eighteenth century, and then North America. Scandinavia became known for striking screen printed fabric yardage during the twentieth century, and design studio Svenskt Tenn and Finnish textile company Marimekko were among the studios who popularized the fabric. Svenskt Tenn was founded in 1924 by Estrid Ericson, who recruited artist Josef Frank to the company, and together they created boldly patterned fabric. Marimekko, a Finnish textile company, was founded by Viljo and Armi Ratia in Helsinki in 1951. Both Scandinavian brands continue to have a striking influence on artists and designers today, especially those who work with screen printing.

DYEING is a method of adding color to cloth by soaking it in a colored substance made from a natural material or chemically formulated dye. Natural dyes are derived from plants, animals, or minerals. The majority of natural dyes are made from plant sources—roots, berries, bark, leaves, wood, and fungi. Most natural dye materials require the use of mordants, which bond the fiber and the dye molecule. Fiber-reactive dyes are chemical dyes formulated to work on natural fibers (cotton, linen, bamboo, hemp, silk), which attach permanently to cellulose fibers using a covalent (electron-sharing) bond. When dyeing, all or only a portion of fabric can be submerged. Dip dye is a method of only submerging a part of a piece of cloth. Methods of "resisting" the dye are ways of creating patterns in the dyed cloth. Resist dyeing involves applying a barrier to block the dye from absorbing in particular areas of the cloth, using materials like wax, mud, string, and bands. Or the barriers are created using folds (simple or complex) in the fabric. Batik is a type of resist dyeing. After the fabric dries completely, the wax is removed. The process of waxing and dyeing can be repeated many times with multiple colors. Tie-dye is a method of folding (or scrunching) resist dyeing. With tie-dye, areas of cloth resist dye because they are bound by materials like string or rubber bands.

Dyeing Traditions

Batik (wax resist) originated in Indonesia, shibori (folding resist) and tsutsugaki (rice paste resist) in Japan and China, tie-dye (folding and banding resist) in East Asia and the United States, bandhani (binding resist) in India, adire eleko (mud resist) in Nigeria, and modrotlač (clay resist) in the Netherlands and Slovakia. Regions that practice batik in Africa use wax resist and also cassava/rice paste for resistant dyeing. Tie-dyeing—or "tied dyeing," as it was more commonly known before the 1960s—is an ancient art practiced across continents and cultures. The essential elements are fabric, string, and colorful dye. Among the oldest tie-dyeing techniques is bandhani, practiced for more than four thousand years in South Asia. Bandhani textiles are produced by plucking fabric into tight, tiny knots before dipping it into dye vats, a method that produces delicate and complicated patterns. Other varied techniques of tie-dyeing were developed in Southeast Asia, South America, and West Africa. Shibori is a Japanese manual tie-dyeing technique that produces a number of different patterns on fabric. Shibori groups resist techniques into three categories: kōkechi (tied or bound), rōkechi (wax), and kyōkechi (folded and clamped between wooden blocks).

Alexis Hartman

Camano Island, Washington
b. 1979

"In my twenties, my relationship with the natural world began to deepen, and plants became my main source of creative inspiration. Translating what I painted into textile design seemed like a natural extension of this inspiration; printing patterns inspired by nature onto fabrics made of plant fibers is a total delight to me."

Alexis Hartman has loved painting since childhood in the Silver Lake neighborhood of Los Angeles. She grew up watching her mother sew and quilt. Hartman inherited her mother's love of cloth, though not sewing. Hartman is deeply inspired by the natural world, primarily the landscape of her native California. She translates patterns from her paintings and hand-carved blocks into silk screens, which she prints onto linen and clay-coated paper. Her printed fabric work is dedicated to the continuous exploration of natural materials and traditional cloth printing techniques. Hartman uses linen from a five-generation, family-owned Belgian manufacturer that upholds a tradition of farm stewardship, natural cultivation, and sustainable production.

Cara Marie Piazza

Manhattan, New York
b. 1989

OPPOSITE AND ABOVE
Dyed fabric bundles using plant matter, minerals, nontoxic metals, and food waste

"I partner with florists and restaurants to take their leftover food waste and plant matter to turn into dye. Our cities need better logistical programming and infrastructure to handle waste, and we need to reimagine how we think of waste, not as trash, but as a resource."

Cara Marie Piazza wanted to work in art and fashion from a young age, growing up in New York City, but was disillusioned with the environmental degradation caused by the fashion industry. Today she creates one-of-a-kind textiles using natural dye materials—plant matter, minerals, nontoxic metals, and food waste. During her thesis year of college at the Chelsea College of Arts in London, Piazza was first introduced to natural dye through a workshop using onion skins. She realized vibrant color could come from plants and was instantly hooked. Piazza uses folding and bundling techniques to control the patterns in her dye cloth. She collaborates with artists and designers, and she teaches workshops on natural dyeing techniques.

Carla Venticinque-Osborn

Crystal Beach, Florida
b. 1979

OPPOSITE
AND LEFT
Hand-stamped
cotton

"My work in textiles allows me to combine my artistry with a viable career. It also provides a platform for practicing ethical business and social policies that I believe in: ensuring fair labor practices, creating job opportunities in disadvantaged communities, promoting sustainability, and supporting the work of handmade artisan communities. As someone who is deeply sensitive and often feels out of step with the fast pace and technological advancements of modern life, working in the handmade crafts and textiles industry has been a grounding experience for me. There's a special kind of beauty in the intricate textures of handworked fabrics, for instance, that speaks volumes about craftsmanship and care."

Carla Venticinque-Osborn is a first-generation American; her mother is from Colombia and her father is from Sicily and Argentina. These cultural roots influence her designs, exploring themes of belonging and renewal alongside patterns influenced by folk arts and ancient motifs. Her label, PO-EM, was founded in 2016 as a way to bridge her designs with heritage production traditions and techniques, working to celebrate and support handmade industries. Venticinque-Osborn works in partnership with established cooperatives and workshops in India, Guatemala, and Mexico. She finds tracing the warp and weft of a textile to be a relaxing experience that soothes anxiety.

Caroline Z Hurley

Brooklyn, New York
b. 1981

OPPOSITE
Oaxaca Sea
Block-printed linen
with water-based ink;
18 × 18–inch
(46 × 46 cm) repeat

ABOVE LEFT
Aquinnah
Block-printed linen
with water-based ink;
54 × 19–inch
(137 × 48 cm) repeat

ABOVE RIGHT
Inkwell
Block-printed linen
with water-based ink;
54 × 21–inch
(137 × 53 cm) repeat

"My great-grandmother, whom I am named after, lived in a small fishing town in Sicily all her life, and I am told she was always sewing. My grandmother always told me I reminded her of her mother, which I always felt flattered by. I do feel like the moment my mother gave me a sewing machine was the day my whole life made more sense. I was in high school, and I immediately started a small business making sewn collaged purses, and from there I started collecting fabrics and never stopped. Textiles feel so IN me—in my blood. While I do identify as a painter, my medium will always be fabrics."

Caroline Z Hurley was born and raised in Memphis, Tennessee, with Italian (Sicilian) grandparents on both sides. As both a designer and painter, her design process has always been rooted in her art practice. She utilizes gestural markings, simple abstractions, and thoughtful use of negative space to create intuitive works that are translated onto the landscapes of textiles and objects. In 2011, Hurley created a homeware company in her name. For years, all of her hand-stamped fabric was made in her Brooklyn studio. Now her block-printed fabric by the yard is printed by artisans in New Bedford, Massachusetts. And her silk-screened fabric is made in collaboration with a family-owned and -operated mill in Rhode Island. In her work with cloth, she feels supported by the women in her life: her grandmother, mother, and sisters.

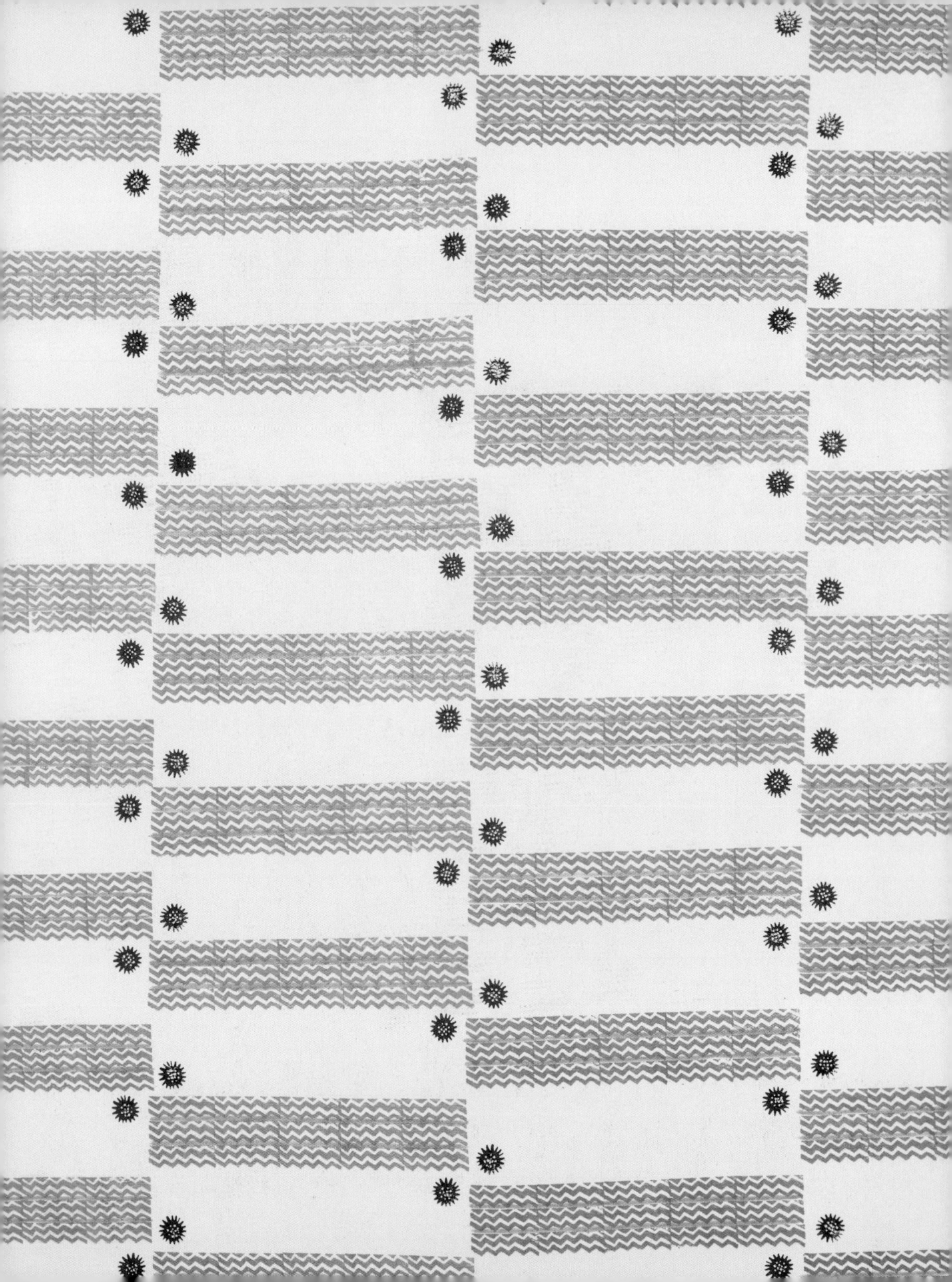

Dalani Tanahy

Mākaha, Oʻahu, Hawaii
b. 1961

"Like all artists who work with raw materials of the earth, there is a combination of awe and humility that grounds me, literally and figuratively. Re-creating the work that my ancestors did makes the experience even more meaningful by connecting me to family, generations past. My work not only supports my life but is tied intrinsically to my culture and identity as a Hawaiian. As part of the revival of a once sleeping art, the teaching component is important to help ensure that kapa-making does not leave our hands again."

As a child, Dalani Tanahy learned to knit, crochet, embroider, and sew. At eighteen, she saw kapa cloth in the Bishop Museum (the Hawaii State Museum of Natural and Cultural History), but it wasn't until age thirty-three that she had direct exposure through a traditional kapa class. The art of Hawaiian kapa had been dormant for sixty years and had recently entered a revival period when Tanahy learned the steps involved in kapa: making cloth using the inner layer of tree bark, carving bamboo printing stamps, following the science of natural dyes and fermentation, and stamping designs onto the bark cloth. Tanahy began her own kapa-making practice, and her kapa cloth has been used for ceremonial repatriations of ancestral remains (returned from museums and universities) and for clothing for hula, weddings, and other traditional Hawaiian ceremonies. She has been teaching kapa-making for twenty-five years.

Emily and Sarah Parkinson

Portland, Oregon (Sarah), and Oakland, California (Emily)
b. 1986 (Sarah), 1989 (Emily)

OPPOSITE
Desert
Screen-printed and
naturally dyed linen

ABOVE
Arches
Screen-printed and
naturally dyed linen

"There's a can-do, creative thread that runs through our family, handed down to us by our mother, and by her mother. It involves textiles, for sure—they both taught us to sew when we were quite young—but it also encompasses a wider range of materials and approaches. Our grandmother was an avid knitter, ceramicist, carpenter, and stained-glass artist. She sewed her entire wardrobe of clothes. Our mother is an illustrator, a painter, a stylist, and a surface designer. She has an incredible eye for color and pattern. We really took away from their examples. More than a love of cloth, our textiles reflect a love of creation."

Sisters Emily and Sarah Parkinson were both drawn to textiles since they were young. Born in Boston, Massachusetts, they learned to quilt and sew in childhood. They find encouragement to keep experimenting and working with textiles within each other. Together, they collaborate on Homebody Textiles, a studio that specializes in naturally dyed and hand-printed cloth goods. Each of their patterns begins as an iterative pencil sketch, which is burned onto a screen and then printed onto cloth with thickened mordants.

Once dyed, the pieces pick up a range of different shades based on the natural dyes used and the ways each one reacts with the various mordants. Every textile goes through at least five to ten separate steps, and every step is a delicate balance between the finicky chemistry of natural dyes and the loose and intuitive work of the artist. They describe a back-and-forth building of ideas at the heart of their textile practice, an easy, yet intense collaboration that evolved out of their first role together—that of sisters.

Gere Kavanaugh

Los Angeles, California
b. 1929

Gere's name (pronounced "Jerry") came up on my phone as I was eating dinner, and I dashed into my office to take the call. It was delightful to speak with her. At age ninety-five, she is sharp and confident. She told me that going to Cranbrook Academy of Art was one of the best things to happen in her life, and she is currently developing her Cranbrook archives. She recalled the many artists with whom she collaborated, while designing interiors for ten Joseph Magnin stores, including three commissions for large hanging sculptures from one of my favorite artists—Ruth Asawa.

—Lena

"My family was Potato Famine Irish. They settled in Bangor, Maine. Then they sailed down to Memphis. My mother taught me about textiles; she taught me how to feel them. She made fabulous clothes for me and my cousins. Once you feel a piece of material, it gets into your blood and your psyche. I'm a designer who designs anything I can get my hands on."

Geraldine "Gere" Kavanaugh was born in Memphis, Tennessee. Her father introduced her to the world of books and botanical prints, and her mother taught her how to create objects from her imagination. This led to being enrolled in art school at the age of eight and continued through high school and beyond. In 1952 Kavanaugh was the third woman to receive an MFA degree from Michigan's Cranbrook Academy of Art. In addition to vibrant printed cloth, Kavanaugh has designed ceramics, light fixtures, store interiors, public art, and furniture. In the 1960s, she founded Gere Kavanaugh Designs and shared studio space with Frank Gehry, Don Chadwick, and Deborah Sussman. Her work epitomized the craft and folk aesthetic of the California design scene in the 1960s and 1970s. Art and design are a way of life for Kavanaugh.

OPPOSITE
The Grammar of Ornament, 1949
Screen-printed cotton

ABOVE
The Seasons, 1970
Screen-printed linen

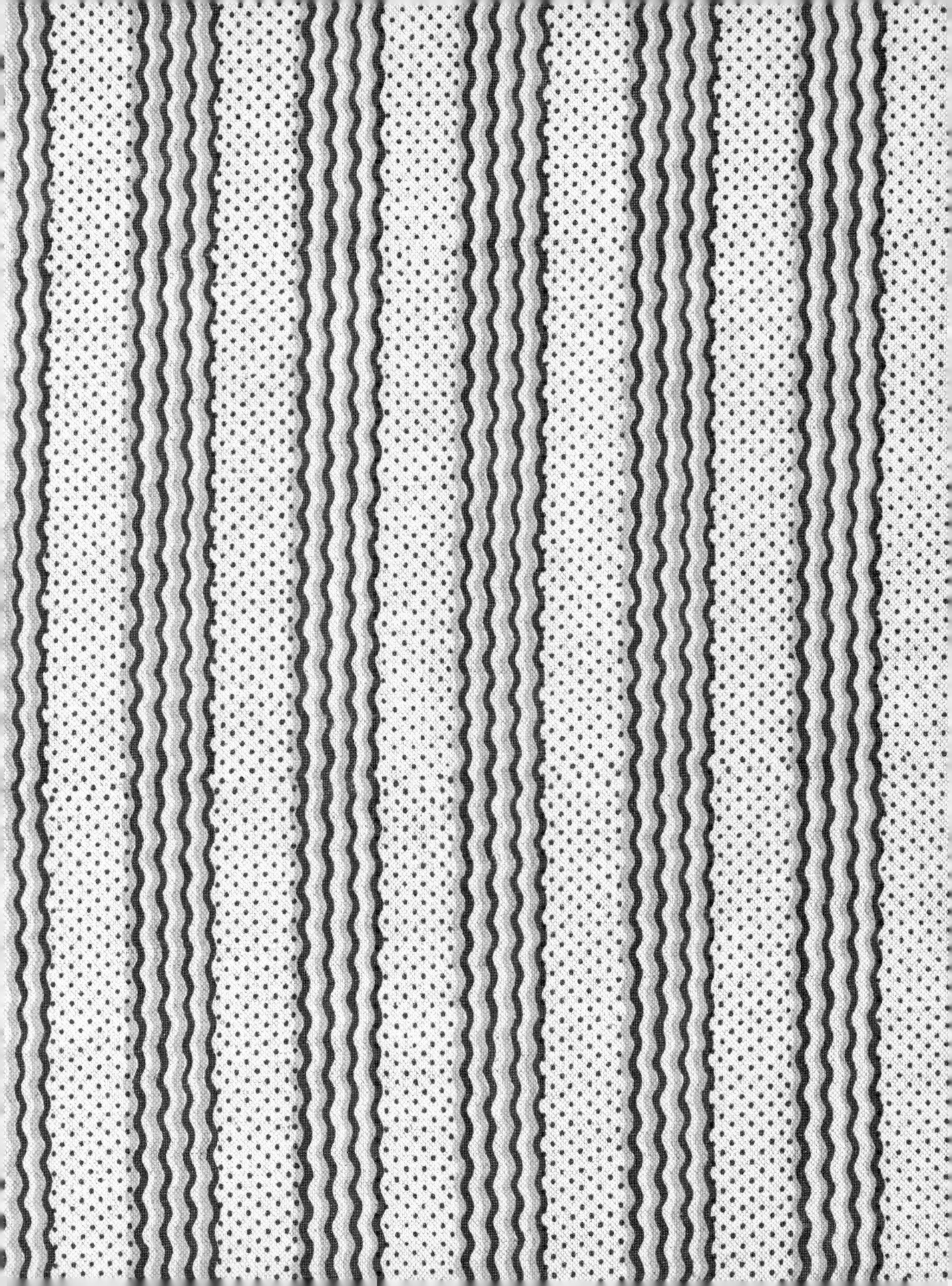

Hopie Stockman Hill

Los Angeles, California
b. 1984

"My grandmother Happy taught me that art is a daily life practice. She was always quilting, sewing, painting furniture, and doing things like adding tomatoes to a bland plate of food in order to make it more interesting and visually appealing. Her quilting group was her passion and core social circle. Every summer growing up I stayed with Happy for two weeks, and we spent the whole time working on elaborate craft projects. She taught me how to sew, needlepoint, quilt, stencil, and cook. Those are some of my happiest childhood memories: listening to old records, chatting, and working with our hands."

Hopie Stockman Hill and her sisters grew up on a farm in New Jersey, painting murals and sewing——thanks to their mother, Lisa. The sisters fell in love with the world of textiles and its intricate, handmade artistic processes. Hopie and her sister Lily founded their textile, art, and design studio, Block Shop, in 2013. They value the slow, collaborative, and considered process of traditional textile methods—collaborating with master block printers in India and Jacquard weavers in Italy. For their block prints, drawings are hand-carved into wooden blocks (each color requiring a different block), and their printers line up the patterns by eye. Stockman Hill and her team draw inspiration from the art and architecture of their surroundings in Southern California. Block Shop is an extension of her daily art practice, which is constantly evolving.

Ilana Kohn

Brooklyn, New York
b. 1981

"My mom has a large framed cross-stitch piece that my great-grandmother made. She stitched it while coming from Europe by boat in 1912. My dad's family all came to the US from Eastern Europe after World War II. We don't know a whole lot about their lives before the war, but I do know that my grandpa was a cobbler in Poland, and when he and my grandma arrived here they both worked in garment factories.

"When I started sewing, my mom got me a sewing machine, but it turned out to be more frustrating than fun. I didn't really get into machine sewing until I was in graduate school, and I bought myself a Pfaff machine that was a pleasure to use."

From a young age, Ilana Kohn loved drawing, painting, and all kinds of craft. As a teenager, in Arlington, Virginia, she reworked thrift store clothing by cutting it up, hand-sewing pieces together, and dyeing the fabric. In college at Pratt Institute in Brooklyn, Kohn studied illustration. After graduating, she worked for nearly a decade as an editorial illustrator. She went back to school to study historic preservation, and at the same time she returned to sewing clothing. She made a batch of dresses and asked a friend to photograph them. Her early collections focused on patterned fabric—marbled and screen printed. Her printed fabric is initially drawn by hand, then transferred to a computer in order to screen print or digitally print yardage. Now her collections use both solid and patterned fabric—knits and wovens. Kohn is proud to create clothing that is sustainable, both in terms of production and economics.

Jason Rosenberg

Brooklyn, New York
b. 1974

OPPOSITE
Allow for the Curvature of the Earth, 2018—present
Beeswax batik and natural dyes on repurposed silk and cotton (detail)

ABOVE
Allow for the Curvature of the Earth

"My great-grandparents worked in the garment industry on the Lower East Side [New York City], so perhaps the desire to hold cloth in my hands is inherent? I think my work is less intentionally rooted in history and tradition, and more intentionally rooted in a personal connection to the earth through observing patterns in nature. But of course it is all connected."

Jason Rosenberg was born in New York City, and he remembers his mother making batiks when he was a child. He loved the color palette and texture of her wall hangings. Since 2013, Rosenberg has spent summers away from Brooklyn on Skomvær, an isolated island at the edge of the Lofoten Islands in Northern Norway/Sápmi, co-running an artist residency and developing his own artistic practice. The geographical remoteness of this Arctic island, its seabird inhabitants, unique geological landscape, tidal current, and unbridled seaweed forests have nourished Rosenberg's artistic vision—and led him to explore his own spiritual relation to the sea and its ecology. From 2016 to 2017 Rosenberg spent time in Indonesia and gained experience with natural dyes and batik. Working with indigo, Rosenberg is in wonder of the infinite shades of blue and how they relate to the Arctic sea surrounding Skomvær. Lately he has been experimenting more with extracting colors from roots, mushrooms, and lichen.

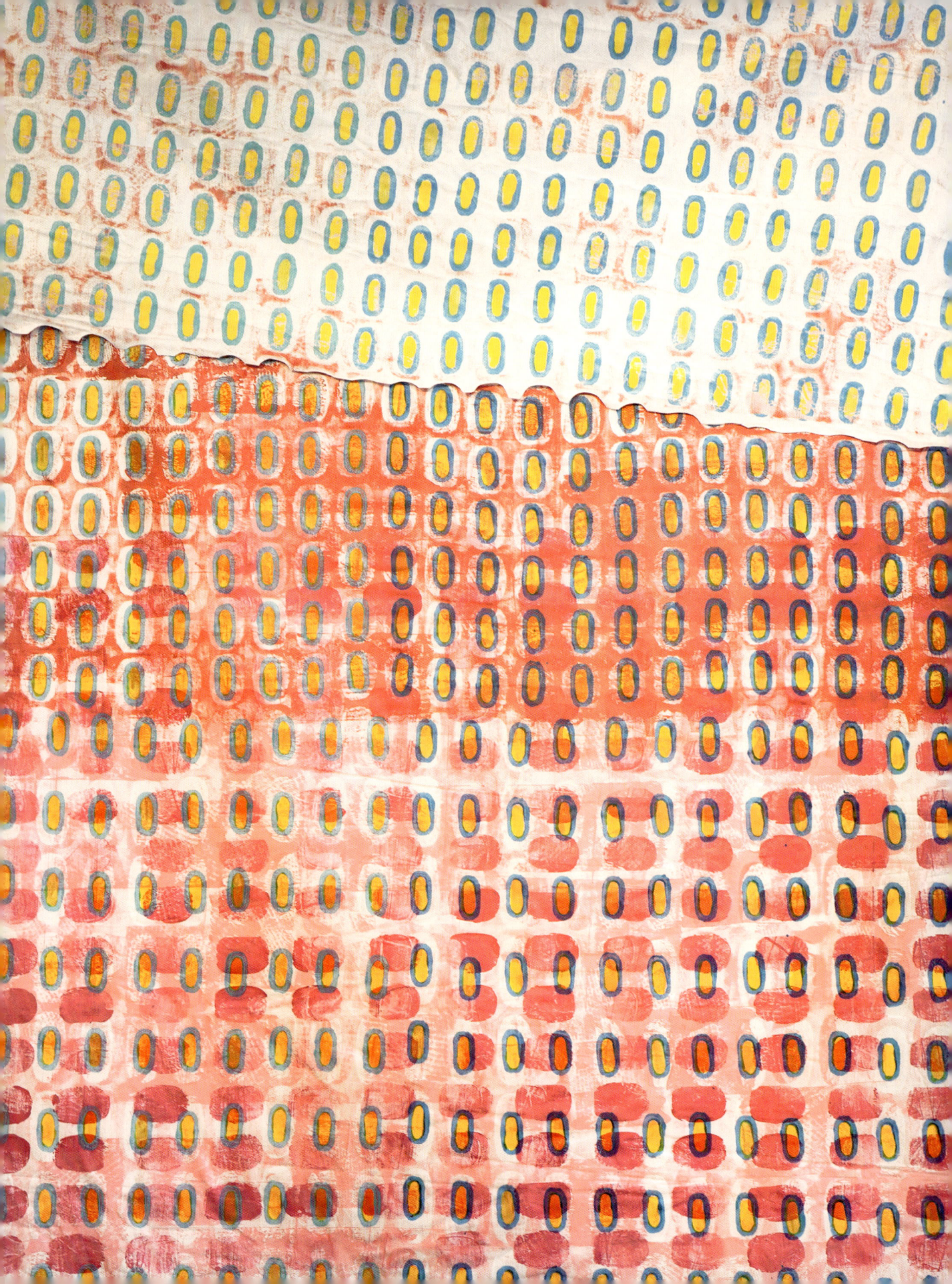

Jeanne Williamson Ostroff

Natick, Massachusetts
b. 1957

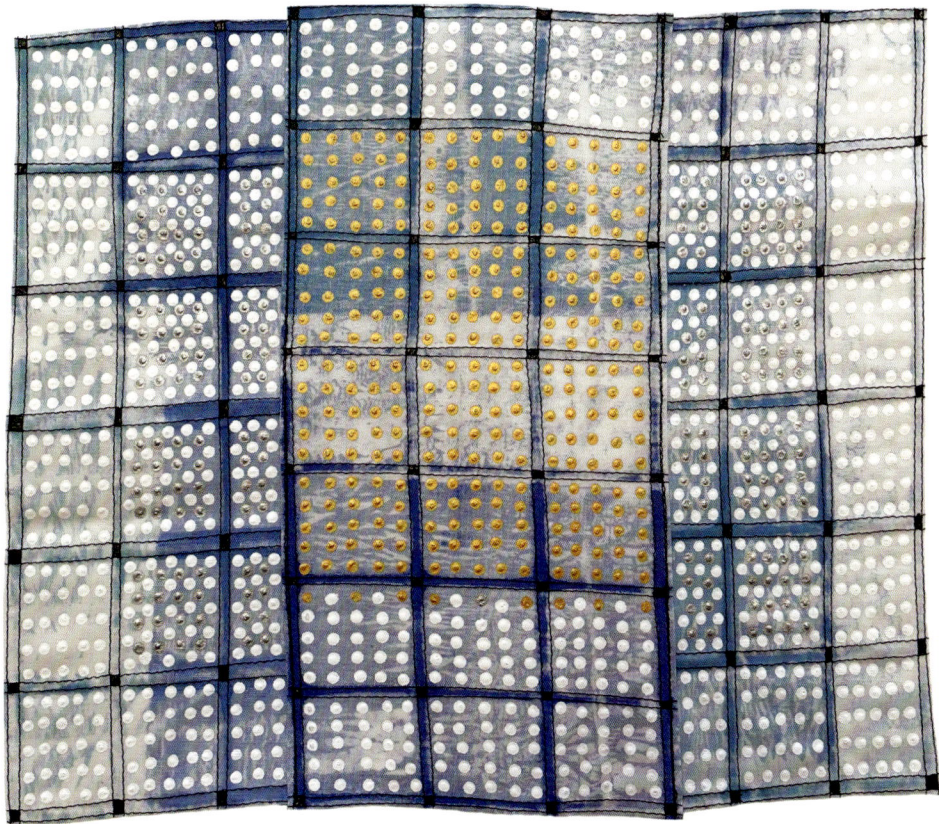

"I have always loved fabric, whether it was clothing, on furniture, or the bolt in a fabric store on upholstery. I made most of my own clothes (shirts, pants, bathing suits, jackets, and coats) from when I was in high school through my early thirties. When my son was born, I made many of his clothes (overalls, pants, coats, raincoats) until he went to kindergarten, because there were few clothing options for boys in the late 1980s unless I wanted to buy clothes with images of trucks, which I did not."

Jeanne Williamson Ostroff has been sewing since she was a child in Philadelphia, Pennsylvania. Her current mixed-media art practice focuses on a combination of print-making, painting, and collage on fabric. Her interest in using construction fences started twenty years ago, when she started noticing different patterns, shapes, and sizes being used as a barrier to keep people safe by blocking off the site. After she monoprints the fence textures on fabric, she also incorporates additional painting and collage techniques. She often stitches the fabric by following the grids of the fence pattern. In her *Loss* series, Williamson Ostroff tells her story of having a mother with untreated mental health issues and how that affected her as a child and as an adult. The monoprinted construction fence fabric is a metaphor for the boundaries she had to set with her mother.

Jen Garrido

San Francisco, California
b. 1974

"I think my calling is to be a painter, but I do love making in general. I wanted space to create and just being a painter felt limiting, so when I landed on fabric, it made so much sense. It felt like a natural way to see lines, shapes, colors, textures, and patterns.

"I have always had an affinity toward thrift stores, flea markets, hunting and finding clothing treasures—and my grandma did too. I learned that from her. I really feel like it's an extension of my creative process. I often take photos of patterns and color combos that I see while hunting for treasures. I love lived-in textures— it is almost like the more it is used, the more I love it as an object to ponder or put in a stack."

Jen Garrido was born in West Los Angeles. She received her BFA in Painting from Sonoma State University and her MFA in Studio Art from Mills College in Oakland. As a painter and textile artist, she navigates between her fine art practice and her work designing and producing printed and overdyed textiles under the name Jenny Pennywood. Garrido begins a textile print by making multiple ink drawings on white paper with a focus on line quality. One pattern emerges through several drawings. Her fabric yardage is screen printed in San Francisco and overdyed north of the city with a family-owned dyehouse. Whether abstract or nature-based, Garrido's work is a focus on color, fluidity, and movement, show-casing forms that sit, lean, lie, or cascade, as one might encounter in nature.

Jen and I share a deep love of printed and dyed fabric. For several years we collaborated on a clothing line focused on these qualities. Jen and I would paint with black ink on white paper, and then scan the artwork to create large repeat patterns in Photoshop. Our fabric was printed at Zoo Ink, one of the few remaining yardage screen printers in the United States. Next, we would drive across the Golden Gate Bridge to have the fabric overdyed by a small family dye business. Jen is still making beautiful goods in this locally focused process. She has an incredible eye for color layering, more expansive and open-minded than my own.

—Lena

OPPOSITE
Checks, Fold, Dashes & Moons
Screen-printed cotton and linen

ABOVE
Triangles
Screen-printed linen; 30½ × 54—inch
(77 × 137 cm) repeat

Kalen Kaminski

New York, New York
b. 1984

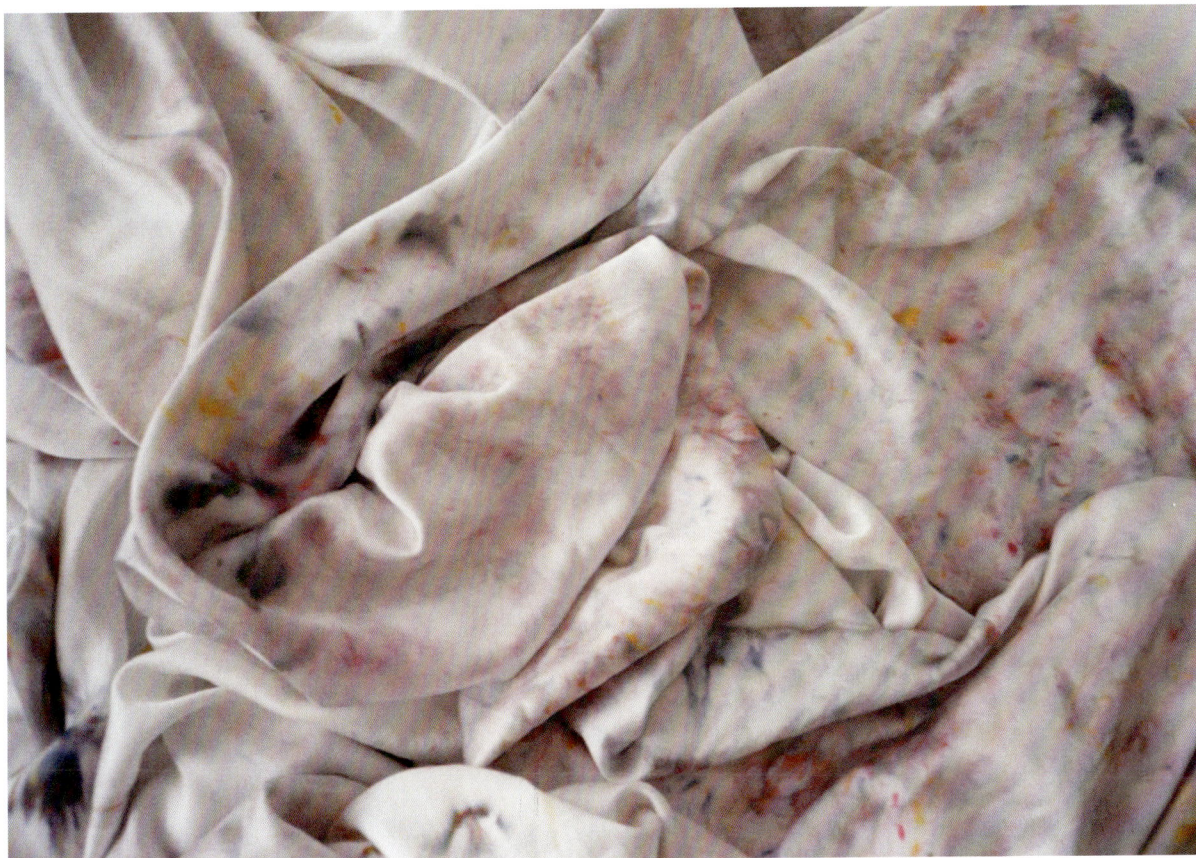

"My grandma Dinny majored in Fashion Design and Textiles. We always connected over textiles, art, and interiors. She started taking me to museums at a young age and, even though I didn't go to school for art, I always felt like I was meant to be making things. I learned by experimenting with new techniques and accidents. I've been doing this for thirteen years and I still feel so connected to it."

Kalen Kaminski lived in Boulder, Colorado, as a child, and spent her time riding horses and doing ballet. She studied anthropology in college and was captivated by textiles from cultures around the world. Kaminski moved to New York City at age twenty-one and began work as a stylist. Her creative brand, Upstate, started as a passion project, while her primary work remained prop styling. Kalen learned intricate shibori techniques from a friend and began with making wraps and scarves. She taught herself through trial and error and expanded to clothing and home goods. Upstate allows her to dynamically engage in the nexus of fashion, art, food, assemblage, and most importantly, communion with her community. Her one-of-a-kind process yields unique, fluid patterns that arise from the beautiful irregularity of hand-dyeing.

Kenya Miles

Baltimore, Maryland
b. 1979

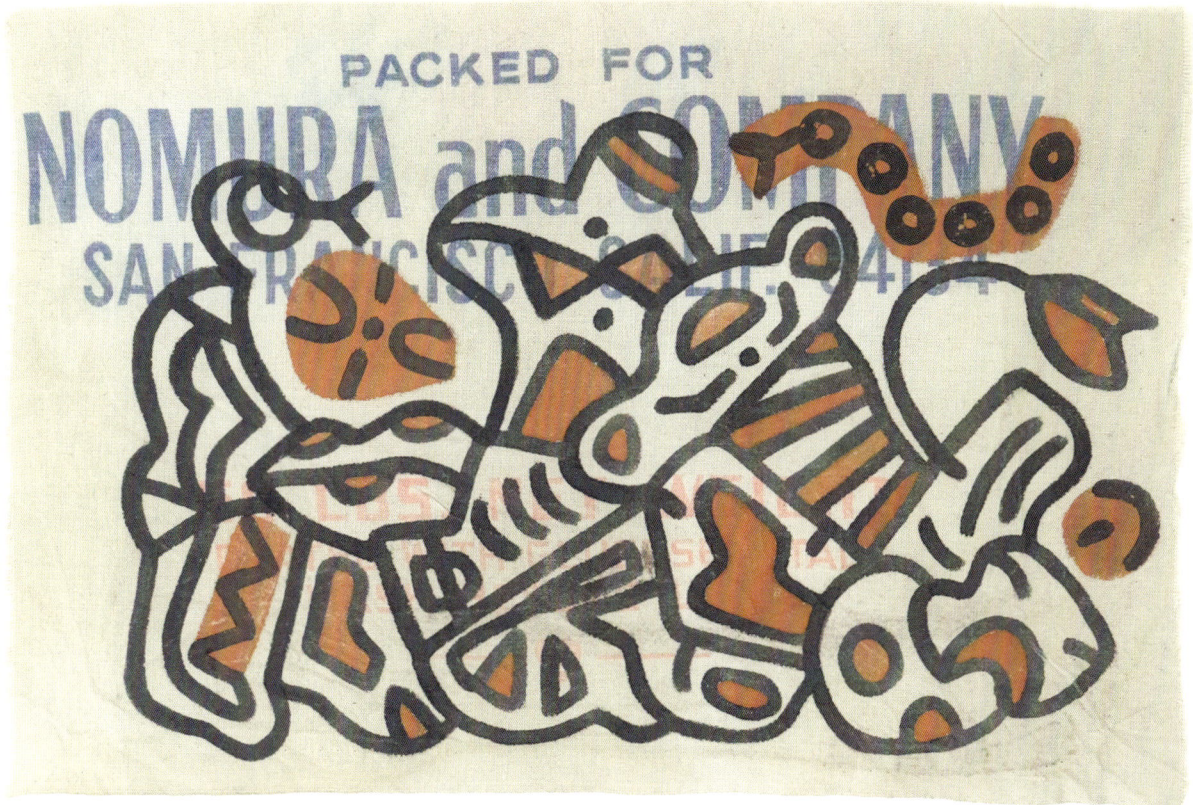

OPPOSITE
Aerial Mapping, 2020
Ngalama-dyed linen
hand-painted with
mud from Mali

ABOVE
Untitled, 2017
Tannin-dyed flour
sack, hand-painted
with soy and earth
pigments

"Every day and every year [at Blue Light Junction] is different, depending on who approaches the studio with ideas. The point is to commune through culture and the cultural lens. What I admire from Gee's Bend and other sewing circles is a continued celebration and a safe space. Without having the attachment to those things in my life, I came to understand that fellowship in other people's cultures and connections. I feel confident in the things I do, and don't, know. I have vision and passion, and I give myself the permission to be in a space of learning."

Kenya Miles is a Baltimore artist and farmer. In January 2020, she founded Blue Light Junction, an alternative color lab, natural dye, garden, and educational facility focusing on growing, processing, and preserving the history of natural dyes and their use on everyday objects. Her vision for Blue Light Junction is a community hub that supports a diverse array of dye projects and intergenerational learning.

In her textile work, Miles uses sustainable materials like earth pigments. Miles's process is a ledger of years of wandering and apprenticing around the globe, from the valleys of Oaxaca, Mexico, to the red clay roads of Ntonso, Ghana. Her work honors ancient practices. She has facilitated workshops at the Berkeley Art Museum, Headlands Center for the Arts, and the UC Berkeley Botanical Garden.

Liz Galbraith and Ephraim Paul

Philadelphia, Pennsylvania
b. 1962 (both)

OPPOSITE
Madras
Hand-block-printed
linen, 18 × 17–inch
(46 × 43 cm) repeat

ABOVE
Ribbon
Hand-block-printed
linen, 18 × 17–inch
(46 × 43 cm) repeat

Liz: "My love of textiles comes from my mother. She hooked rugs, knit sweaters, made quilts, and sewed beautiful dresses for us—and taught me all of these crafts as a child. We traveled when I was growing up, and my mother's search for textiles was always part of the trip. She loved to knit, so we ventured to the Aran Islands for their famous yarn. For her hooked rugs, we visited the long-gone wool merchants of SoHo in New York. The journeys we took to source textiles resonated within me, and sent me on my own path of discovery and creativity."

Married partners Liz Galbraith and Ephraim Paul discovered hand block printing in 1996. Originally from Winnetka, Illinois, they came to Philadelphia after college. As Galbraith & Paul, they design their original patterns, make their printing blocks, mix their palette of colors, and hand block print their fabrics to order. They call their work a labor of love, explaining that hand block printing is the slowest and most simple of printing methods. They employ a staff of twenty in their 4,000-square-foot (373 m) printing studio with eight-yard-long (7.3 m) printing tables. Their process honors traditional techniques while also incorporating their passion for painting and color. Galbraith and Paul have a deep love of craft and feel that designing and printing textiles is a calling.

Lotta Jansdotter

Montclair, New Jersey, and Åland Islands, Finland
b. 1971

OPPOSITE
Tapio (top) and
Abolins (bottom)
Screen-printed linen

ABOVE
Tapio (top left),
Mikko (bottom left),
and *Enda* (top and
bottom right)
Screen-printed linen

"Growing up in Scandinavia, we are constantly reminded of our rich textile history. People use many different kinds of cloth in everyday life, like rya rugs to lay in the boat during boat rides and weavings hung on the wall for insulation on cold winter days. And then we have all the printed fabric. I was surrounded by makers when I grew up. My aunt Kilna was a fashion designer who created her own clothing. My mum loved Marimekko and [everything] was covered in bold prints and patterns."

Lotta Jansdotter grew up in Stockholm, Sweden, where it was mandatory to learn textile arts starting at age nine. She and her classmates had to sew by hand and by machine, as well as embroider. She also watched her mormor (grandmother) mend old jeans and socks, almost never throwing anything away. She has been creating hand-screened fabric accessories and home goods since 1996 and is known for the organic motifs that characterize her designs. Her studio is in historic Manufacturers Village (in East Orange, New Jersey), brick and masonry buildings built in 1880, now comprising more than sixty working-artist spaces. She leads hands-on printmaking workshops and creative retreats, and she is the author of twelve books.

Paige Cleveland

Los Angeles, California
b. 1978

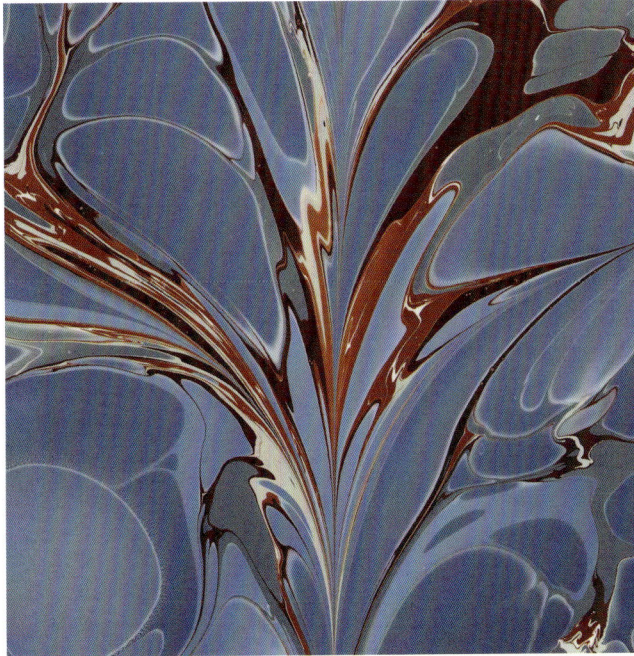

OPPOSITE
Topo
Hand-marbled silk
and cotton twill

LEFT
Stone Plum
Hand-marbled silk
and cotton twill

"Both of my grandmothers had very unique relationships with cloth. My maternal grandmother made beautiful textile art using needlepoint. She always had a piece in progress and made everything from ottomans to wall hangings. She always had her kit nearby and was working on something my whole life. My paternal grandmother was a big collector; she had a huge appreciation for quilt making and commissioned many. She also had a large collection of rugs and blankets from art fairs and markets all over the Mid- and Southwest, many of which I still have."

Paige Cleveland was born in Oklahoma and raised in San Diego, California. Always a tactile person, she was drawn to cloth at a young age. She earned a BFA in Communication Arts from Otis College of Art and Design in Los Angeles. Now, in her downtown Los Angeles studio, she practices traditional methods of dyeing and hand-marbling techniques on silk, linen, cotton, and leather. Cleveland floats and manipulates highly pigmented inks on a liquid surface, then gently and quickly lays cloth on top of the bath to transfer the print. She honors artisan practices while also finding creative exploration in her experimentation. Cleveland first saw marbling demonstrated by artist Jim Anderson while working as a graphic designer (and experiencing a period of professional soul-searching). She then began to experiment with applying marbling techniques to textiles and started her design studio, Rule of Three. Her art practice and relationship with cloth is a union of creative expression, color, and pattern.

Pia Camil

Acatitlan and Mexico City, Mexico
b. 1980

"*My paternal grandfather was from Egypt. He traveled a lot and left Egypt quite young. He graduated from Columbia University, then traveled to Mexico and got involved in politics. He met my grandmother in the north of Mexico and started a cotton plantation [likely with knowledge about Egyptian cotton farming]. My dad, the oldest of seven kids, helped to some extent on the cotton ranch. Where does my fascination with cloth come from? I like to think that there's something connected to my family. My dad always said to me, What are you wearing? What's it made of? He wanted to touch the fabrics. Both my father and grandfather were elegant dressers; they went to bespoke tailors, and I grew up going to tailors.*

"*Now I work with tailors—a group of women, and the head of the [sewing] house is Vicki. We've been collaborating for years. She is an exceptional seamstress; she started sewing at seven years old. Our collaboration became a close friendship. What I learned from her is an intimate relationship that she modeled—mothering and working. I built confidence knowing her, and that bond was very important. She became a collaborator, more than a seamstress. A lot of hands participate in my work.*"

Pia Camil was born and raised in Mexico City. She earned a BFA in Painting from the Rhode Island School of Design and an MFA from the Slade School of Fine Art in London. Drawing and painting were the foundation of her practice before she began her site-specific installations exploring her relation to the urban landscape of Mexico City. Soon after, she engaged in the use of cloth as a primary medium due to its relation to the body as well as its ability to adapt to different contexts depending on where it was sourced. These fabric works are often completed through public participation. By engaging in different collaborative and exchange strategies with the public, she aims to dismantle preconceived ideas of the legacies of modernism and those related to art making and the art market, and to expose dynamics of mass consumption from a feminist perspective.

Rowland and Chinami Ricketts

Bloomington, Indiana
b. 1971 (both)

OPPOSITE
Untitled Noren Partition, 2006
Indigo-dyed hemp kibira, paste resist;
72 × 72 inches
(183 × 183 cm)

LEFT
Noren Partition, 2018
Dyed with light to dark gradation;
64 × 67 inches
(163 × 170 cm)

Rowland: "I remember very happily sitting on my mom's lap learning to use the sewing machine when I was really young."

Chinami: "On festive days my great-grandmother would dress in a special hare-gi kimono before going out. She loved wearing kimono. Looking back now, I believe that part of her love for kimono stemmed from a sense of exaltation, an uplifting of the spirit. When weaving, I think of my great-grandmother, what it means to be Japanese, and all those who employed these same techniques before me."

Rowland Ricketts was born in Connecticut, and Chinami Ricketts in Tokushima, Japan. Together the couple uses natural materials and traditional processes to create their textiles. Rowland first became interested in working with cloth when he learned about natural dyes while living in Japan in the 1990s. Rowland and Chinami met there, over vats of indigo, when they were both apprentices. While Chinami was completing her second apprenticeship in Japan, she and Rowland ran an indigo farm and studio. Now in Bloomington, they live in a house fronted by a field of indigo that is also bordered by their art studios. Rowland ferments the leaves of the indigo harvest several times a summer. He uses it to dye the textiles for his art installations. Chinami handweaves narrow-width yardage for kimono and obi. She spends months of preparation to produce each bolt of fabric.

Samantha Martínez

Oaxaca, Mexico
b. 1990

OPPOSITE
Dyed cotton
poplin and linen/
cotton fabric using
brazilwood (red)
and pericón flower
(yellow)

ABOVE
Dyed linen/cotton
fabric using
brazilwood (red) and
cempasúchil and
brazilwood (orange)

"The context of where I come from is very important, a place with great diversity of artisanal manufacturing, trades, and workshops. I am always attracted to colors, textures, and shapes. Making crafts, using my hands, is a world where I have always felt comfortable and happy. My work is an extension of me: of who I am, what I think, feel, and believe. What I cannot express in words, I express with my hands. It's the deepest connection I have with myself."

Born in Oaxaca, Mexico, Samantha Martínez earned a bachelor's degree in Architecture from the Facultad de Arquitectura, Universidad Autónoma Benito Juárez de Oaxaca. At the same time, she followed her interest in textiles, attending workshops and exhibitions. She learned about the backstrap loom, the pedal loom, natural dyes, indigo dyeing, shibori, cross-stitch embroidery, and embroidery of San Antonino flowers. After finishing her degree, Samantha worked in architecture for five years, then began studying fashion design at the Yakaitian Instituto in Oaxaca, where the knowledge of sewing and pattern-making techniques helped her approach textiles in a new way. When she was twenty-nine, Martínez created her first collection of garments using shibori, natural dyeing, embroidery, and weaving on a pedal loom. She chose the name KOTÓ, inspired by the word *cotón*.

Sasha Duerr

Hawai'i, Hawaii
b. 1975

"I got the opportunity to take a sabbatical from teaching a few years ago, and I traveled to the motherlands on both sides of my family. I went to Malin Head in Northwest Ireland (father's side) and to the dunes of Noordwijk aan Zee, Netherlands (mother's side). I was able to make natural dyes from the local seaweed, salt water, and rose hips of my ancestors—an art and research project I called Great Grandmother Colors.

"Natural dyes have been a way to explore ideas of slow fashion and textiles and also bring people together. I organized social events called Weed Your Wardrobes, focused on rethinking consumption, where participants weed urban community gardens and use those same weeds to dye garments. I also hosted Dinners to Dye For with local farms and slow food chefs—bringing communities together through seasonal meals and using the byproducts of those very same meals for dyeing."

Sasha Duerr grew up living between Maine and Hawai'i. Her parents had a biodynamic farm, and they instilled in Duerr a deep love for plants, ecology, and biodiversity. Duerr centers her practice and research on the collaborative color potential of weeds, food/floral waste, and local/seasonal ingredients. She received a Textiles MFA at the California College of the Arts and taught as part of the Textiles program for more than a decade.

Duerr lectures, consults, and designs curriculum and courses in the intersection of natural color, slow food, slow fashion, and social practice. She loves learning from a wide range of collaborators and mentors who also share her love of plants (chefs, gardeners, ecologists, botanists, perfumers, and herbalists). Duerr is the author of three books: *The Handbook of Natural Plant Dyes*, *Natural Color*, and *Natural Palettes*.

Serena Dugan

Sausalito, California
b. 1973

OPPOSITE
Oletta
Screen-printed linen;
1½ × 3–inch
(3.8 × 7.6 cm) repeat

ABOVE
Cassis
Screen-printed linen;
10 × 8½–inch (25.4 ×
22 cm) repeat

"Textiles throughout the world have a fascinating place: They carry village folklore, are used for wedding dowries, and represent craft traditions that exist only in that village, town, or region. They distinguish place through craft. I believe that printed textiles (my craft) also speak of my time and place. They are time capsules that represent aesthetics of this moment, and my most lyrical form of self-expression."

Serena Dugan takes after her mother, whom she describes as a "great appreciator of textiles." After earning a Psychology degree from Wake Forest University, in North Carolina, Dugan began painting during a year off before graduate school. She pursued her art practice and studied at the Italian International Institute in Florence, Italy. Dugan spent several years working as a decorative painter and realized she wanted to translate her painted patterns onto fabric. She went back to school to study textile design, then created her first line of hand block printed fabrics. Together with entrepreneur Lily Kanter, she launched the textile and furniture company Serena & Lily. Dugan returned to her roots in 2017, spending a few years purely painting. Her printed fabrics under Serena Dugan Studio are an extension of her art practice.

Bleach Printing

Printing is a process of decorating cloth by application of pigments or dyes to the surface. Conversely, a discharge process removes dye to decorate cloth using a bleaching agent. The term "discharge printing," common in fabric and fashion design production, always seemed like an oxymoron to me. But with lovely output! Similar to batik (resist) dyeing, the results yield a soft appearance and touch—no sharp graphic lines compared with screen printing, and no trace feel of ink on the cloth surface. Bleach printing is faster and easier than resist dyeing, making it a fun way to play with repetitive pattern design while embracing the imperfections (splatters) revealed in the process.

MATERIALS

Bottle of bleach

Glass or plastic container, between 3 and 6 inches (7.5 and 15 cm) wide, with a flat bottom

Rags

Dark fabric

Various collected printing tools

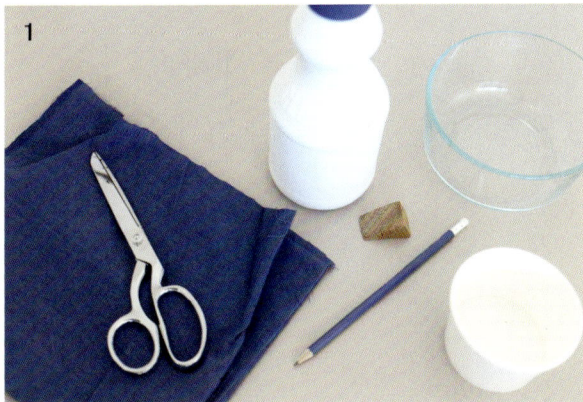

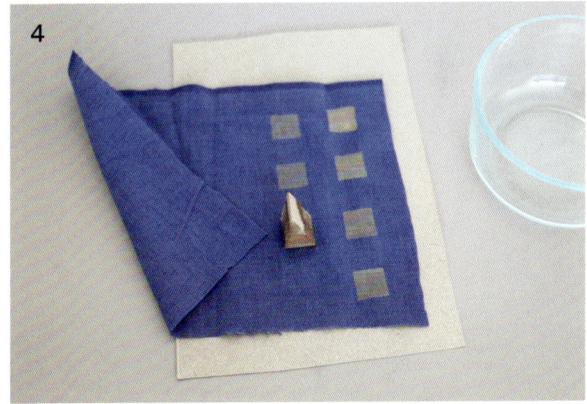

NOTE: *Collect household items that can be dipped into a small dish of bleach and pressed onto fabric. Consider using marker caps, bottle caps, jars, cardboard scraps, and erasers. Choose a work area that is well ventilated, and read the bleach label for safety instructions. Wear clothes that can get messy in the unlikely event that your bleach splashes.*

INSTRUCTIONS

1. Pour a small amount of bleach into your glass or plastic container.

2. Place a rag or piece of cardboard on your work surface, and place a piece of dark fabric on top.

3. In a straight up-and-down motion, dip a printing tool into the bleach. Next, lower the tool onto the dark fabric. Press and hold in place for 2 to 5 seconds. Lift the printing tool and repeat in a new area of fabric.

4. Continue printing, creating a pattern, whether it's horizontal lines, as shown in the examples, or a more free-form style of scattered shapes.

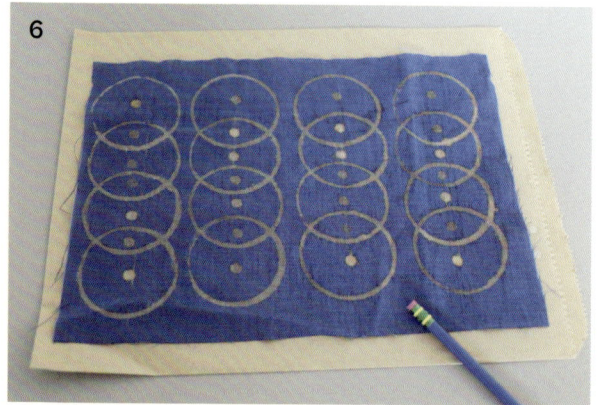

5. Introduce a new printing tool, and add new marks to your design. Watch the bleached areas lighten with time.

6. Experiment with how long a tool is dipped in bleach and how long the tool is pressed to the dark fabric—and observe the results.

7. Consider making a sampler fabric, showing various printing tool results. Additionally, experiment with different fabric types. On linen fabric, bleach can soak along the fiber threads and create the appearance of an ikat pattern.

8. When the bleach fully dries, wash and dry the printed fabric and rags in a separate load of laundry (only necessary for the first wash).

Black Tea Overdyeing

Early in my career, I worked for a textile company owned by British designer Helen Prior. In addition to teaching me how to design complex repeat patterns, she introduced me to the habit of drinking black tea daily. Tea-dyeing is a favorite of mine because of the ease and the resulting warm, chestnut brown tones. White cloth that has gone dingy (napkins, T-shirts, underwear) can be beautifully revived. The term "overdye" means that the dyeing happens after an item has been sewn, compared to dyeing unwoven fibers or fabric yardage. Tea is made with the leaves, stems, and buds of the *Camellia sinensis* plant, and black tea comes in many varieties from different regions—all of which work for dyeing. I use new tea bags for dyeing, but steeped tea bags still have a lot of color in them; used bags can be saved and collected for future dyeing.

MATERIALS

Large soup pot

12 black tea bags, unwrapped from any packaging

¼ cup (60 ml) white or apple cider vinegar (optional)

2–4 fabric items

NOTE: *Tea is rich in tannins that bond with natural fibers, so tea dyeing does not require a mordant (an added substance used to bind the dye to the fabric). Still, I add vinegar to help prevent fading. Natural fibers (cotton, linen, silk, hemp) all take in the color differently, which is part of the fun.*

INSTRUCTIONS

1. Fill the pot with water, to 2 inches (5 cm) from the top. Bring water to a boil.

   Turn off the heat and add the tea bags to the hot water. Let tea bags steep for 15 minutes. Next, use a utensil to remove the tea bags and discard them. Add vinegar, if using, and stir.

2. Place the fabric into the dye bath pot and stir to allow the fabric to get completely submerged.

   A utensil can be placed in a way to keep the fabric fully submerged. Let soak for an hour or more, stirring occasionally.

3. Remove the dyed fabric and rinse it under fresh water until all excess dye is removed and the water runs clear.

4. Wash and dry by machine (separately from other laundry for the first wash only).

Tying Off

I could happily spend another year or more diving deep into the history of cloth and talking with people who immerse themselves in making cloth. Every conversation I've had made me want to learn more. When Pia Camil (page 233) shared the story of her grandfather who moved from Egypt to Mexico and started a cotton farm, I spent time that afternoon reading about the history of Egyptian cotton (a material term I was very familiar with but didn't know much about). My interest has only grown exponentially. While talking (and typing) with contributors, I have kept an open document of quotes that have felt especially resonant. They have helped me put into words my own relationship with cloth. Here are some of them:

The transformation from seed to fiber to fabric feels somewhat magical. When I first learned how to weave on a floor loom and began making fabric, it felt as though a whole world opened up. Textiles have allowed me a greater connection to my heritage and provided a place for me to wrestle with the complexities of familial duties.

—Carolina Jiménez

. . .

I believe all humans share an innate, ancestral bond with fibers and textiles. My deep appreciation for handmade textiles may stem from a primal urge to connect with my human past through these threads. Reflecting on my Mediterranean and Latin heritage shapes my designs and serves as a key source of inspiration in my textile work.

—Carla Venticinque-Osborn

. . .

As a teacher and professor I have borne witness to so many talented souls and their creative ideas and projects with cloth. There is not one way. We can begin now, right where we are—being creative with what we have in our own individual lives, connecting with our communities, rethinking methods of art and design, and supporting each other in our efforts. This inspires me deeply.

—Sasha Duerr

I've come to understand so many things about life through working with cloth. It has formed the essential question I ask every artist I talk with: "How has working with cloth made you more human?" I'm still working on my own personal answer to that question, but for me, textiles teach me a lot about interconnectedness, the warp and weft of all living things.

—Zak Foster

. . .

Knitting itself is such a time for meditation and reflection. I think of my dad (who passed away ten years ago now) and my grandmothers. This skill of knitting is something I will always have. It is mine, and it was a gift. I hope they know how much it means to me.

—Anna Wallack

. . .

"A family friend was skeptical about my decision to attend art school. He suggested that it might be a foolish career path. Because I was financially responsible for paying my way through college, I followed my own interests despite a lack of encouragement. I have never looked back with any regret, and my decision has allowed me to build a weaving-centered life. I have many friends and family members enthusiastically cheering me on now."

—Susie Taylor

In these quotes I see some themes, including finding connection to the past and keeping ancestral traditions alive, a pure joy and sustained interest in handwork, and experiencing meaning through creative expression together in community.

Last year I went to an event for author Ocean Vuong, who was on a book tour for *Time Is a Mother*. Vuong explained that he often imagines himself navigating a boat alone when he writes. When he looks back at the shore, he sees all of his ancestors—mother, grandmother, and rows of relatives extending behind them. He acknowledges that he is only here now because of their prior lives. As I have worked on this book, I have held in mind my relatives and ancestors working with cloth, and those of all the contributors—especially for the artists who are reviving techniques lost for generations.

When I asked each contributor about their interest in cloth and work by hand, so many said that it started at a very young age, and I nodded with recognition. My favorite activity as a child was always art. From my observation, all children enjoy making art, and some of us never stop. We feel a pull, deep in our psyche, to express ourselves through work with our hands. It takes some bravery to continue making art into adulthood.

Finally, ways of being in community came up often in responses: teaching, leading and attending artist residencies, participating in sewing circles, creating online communities, and involving the public with their art practices. I heard stories of emotional support and bolstered activism created in these communities. One artist told me she joined a weaving group with stubborn reluctance, and it turned out to be life-changing. While this has helped answer my question—why cloth?—another important piece is simply that I have a choice. I'm aware of the privilege I'm afforded in being able to follow my passions and interests freely. Still, as I started this book project, I was in a phase of life where I was doing much less of my favorite thing: crafting with my hands. Over the past decade, having time to dive deep into an experimental and involved project felt out of reach. But in the process of making this book, I have felt so inspired to get back to cloth projects big and small. I'm going to make the time, and I cannot wait.

Acknowledgments

Thank you, to:

Lee Jensen, Chloe May Brown, Ariel Clute, Stephanie Congdon Barnes, Wendy Van Wagner, Chau Nguyen, Claire Wolfe Boockmeier, Jane Loeser, Serrana Laure Gay, and Jeff Canham
—for their creative support.

Amy Reid Hirst, Michelle Yi Martin, Lacey Segal, Ivan Iannoli, Sherise Lee, Jessica Battilana, Rachel Kaye, Tia Cole, Jenny Shaw, Sarah Maher Storella, Sarah Borruso, Courtney Masterson, Sarah Donahue, Jenny Trotter, Raïssa Bump, Maria Vettese, Outer Sunset Plunge Crew, and GOTV Moms
—for their friendship and checking in.

Shawna Mullen, Hannah Braden, Jenice Kim, and the team at Abrams
—for encouragement and making beautiful books.

Erin Kunkel, Mariko Reed, Nicole Franzen, Rebecca Chotkowski, John Gruen, Stacy k. Allen, Aya Brackett, Ashley Hafstead, Brian Guido, Jennifer Cheung, and David Studarus
—for their beautiful photographs.

Neal Taylor, Kacey Bejado, Louise Mara Sandhaus, Verónica Valdés Vega, Mary Jane Bolton, Chessa Osburn, Edurni Diaz, and Poppy Trived
—for giving their time.

My husband, Josh Dreier; my children, Eli and Abe; my brothers and sisters-in-law, Eddie, Max, Alicia, and Cynthia; and my parents, Patty and Blade
—for helping create time and space for me to work, and for their love.

OPPOSITE
Photo of Travis Meinolf by Lena Corwin

Artist Credits

Weave and Braid

Alice Adams (pages 16—17)
Courtesy of David Hall Gallery
Photographs: Will Howcroft Photography

Brent Wadden (pages 18—19)
Courtesy of Peres Projects

Carolina Jiménez (pages 20—21)
Courtesy of the artist
Portrait photograph: Sophie Fabbri

Cassandra Mayela Allen (pages 3 and 22—23)
Courtesy of the artist
Portrait photograph: Josefina Santos

Christy Matson (pages 24—25)
Photographs: Joshua White

Clare Hu (pages 26—27)
Courtesy of the artist

Dana Haim (pages 28—29)
Photographs: Jessica Kassin

Debra Sparrow (pages 30—31)
Woven blanket:
Photograph: Tim Bonham
Courtesy of The Museum of Anthropology at the University of British Columbia
Wall hanging:
Photograph: Jessica Bushey
Courtesy of The Museum of Anthropology at the University of British Columbia

Elise McMahon (pages 32—33)
Courtesy of the artist

Federico Chávez Sosa and Dolores Santiago Arrellanas (pages 34—35)
Courtesy of the artists

Isa Rodrigues (pages 36—37)
Photographs: Lynn Hunter

James Bassler (pages 38—39)
Courtesy of Browngrotta Arts

Jovencio de la Paz (pages 40—41)
Courtesy of the artist

Kelly Harris Smith (pages 42—43)
Courtesy of the artist

Marina Contro (pages 44—45)
Courtesy of the artist

Michelle Yi Martin (pages 46—47)
Courtesy of the artist and Municipal Bonds gallery

Rachel DuVall (pages 48—49)
Photographs: Carmen Chan for *Cereal* magazine

Rachel Meginnes (pages 50—51)
Courtesy of the artist

Rachel Snack (pages 52—53)
Courtesy of the artist

Rhiannon Griego (pages 54—55)
Courtesy of the artist
Portrait photograph: Ashley Hafstead

Sheila Hicks (pages 4 and 56—57)
Courtesy of Sikkema Jenkins & Co.

Susana Vicente Galan (pages 58—59)
Courtesy of Twenty One Tonnes
Photographs: Rosalinda Olivares

Susie Taylor (pages 60—61)
Courtesy of the artist

Travis Meinolf (pages 62—63)
Photographs: Lena Corwin

Sew and Quilt

Adam Pogue (pages 74—75)
Courtesy of Blunk Space gallery and the artist

Anthony Akinbola (pages 4 and 76—77)
Courtesy of Night Gallery, Los Angeles

Blair Saxon-Hill (pages 78—79)
Courtesy of Nino Mier Gallery and the artist

Cassie McGettigan (page 80—81)
Photographs: Sibila Savage

Denyse Schmidt (pages 82—83)
Photographs: John Gruen

Doris Pettway Mosely (pages 84—85)
Photographs: Stacy k. Allen

Elizabeth Brandt (pages 86—87)
Courtesy of the artist

Faith Ringgold (pages 88—89)
Slave Rape #2 © 2024 Faith Ringgold / Artists Rights Society (ARS), New York, courtesy Pippy Houldsworth Gallery, London, photographed by Tom Powel Imaging; *Subway Graffiti #2* © 2024 Faith Ringgold / Artists Rights Society (ARS), New York, courtesy Pippy Houldsworth Gallery, London, photographed by Benjamin Westoby

Jonathan Parker (pages 90—91)
Courtesy of the artist

Kathryn Clark (pages 92—93)
Courtesy of the artist; portrait photograph: Rebecca Chotkowski

Kiva Motnyk (pages 94—95)
Courtesy of Egg Collective
Photographs: Nicole Franzen

Kristen Lombardi (pages 96—97)
Photographs: Erin Kunkel

Magnus Maxine (pages 98—99)
Courtesy of the artist

Mansur Nurullah (pages 100—101)
Courtesy of the artist

Maura Ambrose (pages 102—103)
Courtesy of the artist

Meg Callahan (pages 104—105)
Courtesy of the artist

Michael A. Cummings (pages 106—107)
Courtesy of the artist

Niki Tsukamoto (pages 108–109)
Courtesy of the artist

Patricia Gorelangton (pages 110–111)
Photographs: Mariko Reed

Pauline Boyd (pages 112–113)
Courtesy of Oroboro

Rachel Meade Smith (pages 114–115)
Courtesy of the artist

Sarah Nsikak (pages 116–117)
Photographs: Trey Millward

Season Evans (pages 118–119)
Courtesy of the artist

Sharon Pettway Williams (pages 120–121)
Photographs: Stacy k. Allen

Zak Foster (pages 122–123)
Courtesy of the artist

Loop and Felt

Akiko Kotani (pages 138–139)
Photographs: Seliná Roman

Angela Hennessy (pages 140–141)
Courtesy of pt. 2 Gallery and the artist

Anna Wallack (pages 142–143)
Courtesy of Misha & Puff

Channing Hansen (pages 144–145)
Courtesy of Marc Selwyn Fine Art

Daphne Chen (pages 146–147)
Photographs: Erik Gould

Debra Weiss (pages 148–149)
Photographs: David Studarus

ektor garcia (pages 150–151)
Courtesy of the artist and Rebecca Camacho Presents, San Francisco
Photographs: Robert Divers Herrick

Emily Holtzman (page 152–153)
Courtesy of the artist

Emily Nora O'Neil (pages 4 and 154–155)
Courtesy of the artist

Jennifer Berg (pages 156–157)
Courtesy of the artist
Jessica Switzer Green (pages 156–157)
Courtesy of JG Switzer

Josh Faught (pages 160–161)
Courtesy of the artist

Karen + Marie Potesta (pages 162–163)
Courtesy of Micaela Greg

Kristina Foley (pages 164–165)
Courtesy of the artist

Lindsay Degen (pages 166–167)
Photographs: Kate Foster & John Hesselbarth

Melissa Dadourian (pages 168–169)
Courtesy of the artist

Micah Clasper-Torch (pages 170–171)
Courtesy of the artist

Pauline Shaw (pages 172–173)
Courtesy of the artist

Rose Pearlman (pages 174–175)
Courtesy of the artist

Sagarika Sundaram (pages 176–177)
Courtesy of the artist

Tanya Aguiñiga (pages 178–179)
Courtesy of the artist

Tracy Krumm (pages 180–181)
Photographs: Tal Wilson

Trish Andersen (pages 182–183)
Courtesy of the artist

Windy Chien (pages 184–185)
Courtesy of Studio Windy Chien
Photographs: Molly DeCoudreaux

Print and Dye

Alexis Hartman (pages 198–199)
Courtesy of Lake August

Cara Marie Piazza (pages 200–201)
Courtesy of the artist

Carla Venticinque-Osborn (pages 202–203)
Courtesy of the artist

Caroline Z Hurley (pages 204–205)
Courtesy of the artist

Dalani Tanahy (pages 206–207)
Courtesy of the Hawai'i State Foundation on Culture and the Arts and Donkey Mill Art Center

Emily + Sarah Parkinson (pages 208–209)
Courtesy of the artists

Gere Kavanaugh (pages 210–211)
Photographs: Jennifer Cheung, previously published in Louise Sandhaus and Kat Catmur, *A Colorful Life* (New York: Princeton Architectural Press, 2019); portrait photographs: Brian Guido, previously published in Sandhaus and Catmur, *A Colorful Life*

Hopie Stockman Hill (pages 212–213)
Courtesy of Block Shop

Ilana Kohn (pages 214–215)
Courtesy of the artist

Jason Rosenberg (pages 216–217)
Courtesy of the artist

Jeanne Williamson Ostroff (pages 218–219
Courtesy of the artist

Jen Garrido (pages 4 and 220–221)
Courtesy of the artist

Kalen Kaminski (pages 222–223)
Courtesy of the artist

Kenya Miles (pages 224–225)
Courtesy of the artist

Liz Galbraith and Ephraim Paul (pages 226–227)
Courtesy of Galbraith & Paul

Lotta Jansdotter (pages 228–229)
Courtesy of the artist

Paige Cleveland (pages 230–231)
Courtesy of Rule of Three

Pia Camil (pages 232–233)
Photograph: Sam Kahn, courtesy of Poe Gallery

Rowland and Chinami Ricketts (pages 234–235)
Courtesy of Ricketts Indigo

Samantha Martínez (pages 236–237)
Courtesy of the artist

Sasha Duerr (pages 238–239)
Photographs: Aya Brackett

Serena Dugan (pages 240–241)
Courtesy of the artist

About the Author

Lena Corwin (b. 1977, San Francisco) was raised among artists in her family and greater community. She attended University of Oregon with a focus on Art History and Women's Studies. Corwin began her career as a graphic and textile designer for fashion companies in New York, concurrently continuing her education taking art and design courses. For several years she taught craft classes from her Brooklyn studio. Since returning to California, she has launched personal projects and expanded her client projects and collaborations. She works with a wide range of handmade techniques and uses computer technology as a complementary tool. She is the author of *Printing by Hand* (2008) and *Made by Hand* (2013), both published by Abrams. She lives in the Outer Sunset neighborhood of San Francisco.

OPPOSITE TOP
Lena Corwin, 2024

OPPOSITE BOTTOM LEFT
Lena Corwin, 1979 (with maternal grandmother)

OPPOSITE BOTTOM RIGHT
Lena and Wolf Seitchik, 1934 (maternal great-great-grandparents)

Editor: Shawna Mullen
Designer: Jenice Kim
Managing Editors: Logan Hill and Lisa Silverman
Production Manager: Alison Gervais

Library of Congress Control Number: 2024942962

ISBN: 978-1-4197-7326-6
eISBN: 979-8-88707-261-6

Other photograph credits:
page 2: *Maps of Displacement: East Coast*, 2023, Cassandra Mayela Allen
page 4: Sheila Hicks (top left); Anthony Akinbola (top right);
Emily Nora O'Neil (bottom left); Jen Garrido (bottom right)

Excerpt on page 17 from interview by Jonathan D. Lippincott for the American Abstract Artists
organization, May 1, 2022, is reprinted with permission courtesy of Jonathan D. Lippincott.
Excerpt on page 91 from interview by Osei Bonsu for *frieze* magazine, 2018, is reprinted
with permission courtesy of Osei Bonsu.

Printed and bound in Malaysia
10 9 8 7 6 5 4 3 2 1

Abrams books are available at special discounts when purchased in quantity
for premiums and promotions as well as fundraising or educational use.
Special editions can also be created to specification. For details, contact
specialsales@abramsbooks.com or the address below.

ABRAMS The Art of Books
195 Broadway, New York, NY 10007
abramsbooks.com